RAZING THE BASTIONS

HANS URS VON BALTHASAR

RAZING THE BASTIONS:

ON THE CHURCH IN THIS AGE

With a Foreword by
Bishop Christoph Schönborn, O.P.

Translated by Brian McNeil, C.R.V.

COMMUNIO BOOKS

IGNATIUS PRESS   SAN FRANCISCO

Title of the German original:
Schleifung der Bastionen:
Von der Kirche in Dieser Zeit
© 1952 Johannes Verlag, Einsiedeln
Published with ecclesiastical approval

Cover art: *Conquest of Jericho*, S. Maria Magiore, Rome
Scala/Art Resource, New York, K25232

Cover design by Roxanne Mei Lum

CONTENTS

FOREWORD

Hans Urs von Balthasar himself described *Razing the Bastions* as a "programmatic little book",[1] and it has also been broadly understood as such. This captivating book, written with passionate verve, was very often set in opposition to von Balthasar's later development in the years after the Second Vatican Council. *Razing the Bastions* was seen as presenting the program of a Christianity open to the world, whereas after the Council von Balthasar was considered to have sounded the trumpet for the Church to retreat into the inner room. It cannot be the business of this short foreword to take a position in such polemics, distributing labels like "progressive" or "conservative", defending the book or locating it "politically". It is more important to hear again, and afresh, the summons to "raze the bastions" and to meet *today* the claim formulated here.

Razing the Bastions pleads for a Church that interprets the "signs of the age", grasps them and answers them, allowing herself to be awakened by the (Holy) Spirit and by the age "from the bed of

[1] "In Retrospect" in *My Work: In Retrospect* (San Francisco: Ignatius Press, 1993), p. 51.

historical sleep for the deed of today" (p. 37).[2]
What the age requires and the Spirit urges is "the
descent of the Church into contact with the
world" (p. 99). This is not a demand imposed on
the Church only from the outside. Certainly the
medieval congruence of the world with the inner
room of the Church is shattered. The Church
stands as one body among many others. The modern age has made us inexorably aware of the multi-
plicity of religions, and it has also smashed the
closed form of Christianity through the division in
faith among Christians themselves. The Baroque
period wished to restore once again the totality of
the Catholic world. "The splendor of this salvage
attempt has passed away" (p. 51). The restoration
in the nineteenth and twentieth centuries conceals
the extent of the crisis (p. 17). Thus the alert
Christian today must "attempt, painstakingly and
gropingly . . . , to interpret the plans of Providence for the Church in today's world" (p. 51).

Whither is the Spirit driving the Church, what
is he saying to the Bride (Rev 2:7; 22:17)? A "new
Catholic attitude" must be learned (p. 52), one
must "plot the course of the shift in Christian
awareness since the middle ages" (p. 68); it is a
question, involving "a mysterious audacity and an
apparent paradox" (p. 52), of understanding
today's situation of the Church in the world as a
"new situation of solidarity" (p. 52). It is a ques-

[2] These page references refer to the pages of this volume.

tion of "the idea of fellowship in destiny, the dominating idea in our age" (p. 68), of "an ever deeper and more serious incarnation" of the Church in the world (p. 71). The Christian can no longer "from the highest watchtower atop the world-cone, look out, *oneself unmoving*, at all the movement . . . ; one must *set oneself in motion*" (pp. 72–73). The "new function of the Church" is to be the "yeast of the world" (p. 62); she must understand herself as "the instrument of the mediation of salvation to the world" (pp. 54–55). The Church as a whole experiences the situation of the diaspora today. "This is the moment when for the first time responsibility for the world and apostolate takes hold of every member of the Church as something self-evident" (p. 62). "Today there is no doubt that the hour of the laity is sounding in the Church" (p. 38). This, in key phrases, is the "program".

Von Balthasar himself pointed out, in a conversation with Angelo Scola in 1985, that the Second Vatican Council ("naturally without regard to me") "adopted" much of this program and "deepened it and taught it". In this same conversation, von Balthasar also said, with unmistakable clarity, that he still stands fully by the contents of *Razing the Bastions*.[3] How is it then that his statements from the period after the Council were felt by

[3] *Test Everything: Hold Fast to What Is Good* (San Francisco: Ignatius Press, 1989), p. 13.

many to be opposed to his book of 1952? Had von Balthasar changed course in the interval? Had he experienced himself, now that many of his ideas had been taken up by the Council, a measure of anxiety in face of his own courage?

In *Rechenschaft 1965* ("In Retrospect"), the sixty-year-old von Balthasar explained what was often interpreted as a turning away from his earlier openness to the world. He writes there:

> At that time came my programmatic little book *Razing the Bastions*, the final and already impatient blast of the trumpet calling for a Church no longer barricaded against the world. The blast did not die away unheard, but now it forced the trumpeter himself to reflect more deeply.
>
> Indeed it was not as though we were unaware that with an opening to the world, an *aggiornamento*, a broadening of the horizons, a translation of the Christian message into an intellectual language understandable by the modern world, only half is done. The other half—of at least equal importance—is a reflection on the specifically Christian element itself, a purification, a deepening, a centering of its idea, which alone renders us capable of representing it, radiating it, translating it believably in the world.[4]

And then he writes, with unmistakable clarity:

> The last ten years have shown inexorably that the most dynamic [Christian] program of openness to the world remains one-sided (and hence becomes exceedingly dangerous) if it does not cultivate with growing awareness its own distinctive counterpoise and balance: whoever

[4] "In Retrospect" in *My Work: In Retrospect*, p. 51.

desires greater action needs better contemplation; whoever wants to play a more formative role must pray and obey more profoundly; whoever wants to achieve additional goals must grasp the uselessness and futility, the uncalculating and incalculable (hence "unprofitable") nature of the eternal love in Christ, as well as of every love along the path of Christian discipleship . . . .

Every program of mission to the world must at all times contain what Guardini called "the discernment of what is Christian" (p. 52).

. . . For this reason, lest everything in the Church become superficial and insipid, the true undiminished program for the Church today must read: the greatest possible radiance in the world by virtue of the closest possible following of Christ (pp. 57–58).

"The discernment of what is Christian"—this could serve as the heading for much of what von Balthasar wrote after the Council, for example his *Elucidations*, his *Moment of Christian Witness*, his *Christian Meditation*.[5] But this concern is not at all new in von Balthasar. In a certain sense, the "discernment of what is Christian" is the fundamental trait of his whole oeuvre, from the *Apocalypse of the German Soul* (1937–1939) onward. When, with inconceivable intensity and breadth, he questions writers from the classical period to the present day—poets, mystics, philosophers and theologians—about their "ultimate attitudes", what is at

---

[5] *Elucidations* (London: Society for Promoting Christian Knowledge, 1975), *The Moment of Christian Witness* (New York: Newman Press, 1968), *Christian Meditation* (San Francisco: Ignatius Press, 1989).

stake is always the question Christ poses to each man in a wholly unique, unmistakably personal way: "But you, who do you take me to be?" (Mk 8:29). Discernment is essential: what is involved is the decision that determines one's life: "Whoever confesses me in the presence of men, I will also confess him in the presence of my Father in heaven" (Mt 10:32).

Von Balthasar's oeuvre is a passionate confession of faith in what is central: in Christ as "the power of God and the wisdom of God" (1 Cor 1:24), in "Christ who was crucified, a stumbling block for the Jews, folly to the Gentiles" (1 Cor 1:23).

> For the Christian this event forms the very center of existence, and he sees everything of any consequence in this world as gravitating toward it. . . . For the Christian there is no "neutral" form of existence, which is not affected or illuminated by the mystery of absolute love, and whose fortuitous and doubtful nature is not justified or made meaningful by it. . . . Why? Because God became flesh (*Moment of Christian Witness*, p. 30).

flesh that was visible, tangible, bodily and therefore unavoidably concrete. The appearing "of the goodness and love for men of God our Savior" (Titus 3:4) brings history and every individual into a situation of decision. Von Balthasar developed this theme not only in his works on the theology of history; unwearyingly and up to the very close of his life, in numerous retreats in the spirit of Saint Ignatius, he also helped people to make the decision of faith for Christ, the "discernment" in their choice of life: "Here . . . is what it means to be a Christian in its 'primordial' sense: effective hearing of the Word who calls and growth in freedom for the expected response" (*My Work*, p. 52).

Von Balthasar's closeness to the Reformation too lies in this pointing toward the obedience of faith, practiced in the retreats and reflected upon repeatedly in the theological work. He says this himself: "It is here, too, that we came closest to the sense and inspiration of the Reformation, from Luther to Karl Barth" (ibid.). Too little attention, in my opinion, has been paid as yet to the supreme significance of von Balthasar's work for a profound reception of the "inspiration" of the Reformation. Here lies a great ecumenical task waiting to be done!

But the "discernment of what is Christian" also means enduring and embodying the whole breadth of what is Catholic: to affirm and to know the fullness of the tradition, without which the Church would not be the *Catholic* Church, and at the same time to have the power "to grasp clearly today's mission for the Church of today's times, and to tackle this mission without succumbing to exhaustion" (p. 44 of the present book). Such breadth makes tremendous demands: "Does not experience show that the personalities capable of managing both tasks are sown so thinly that one can only consider them exceptions?" (p. 44). Von Balthasar belonged without doubt to this group. When one looks back, one may say that, in a supreme and exemplary manner, in his writing and in his activities, he himself incarnated the "program" of a Catholicity without defensive bastions.

Von Balthasar continually demanded the "discernment of what is Christian" as a claim against an *aggiornamento* that threatens to dissolve precisely what is centrally Catholic by relativizing it pluralistically and making it an arbitrary matter of language games. Naturally, such unambiguity has nothing in common with the "integralism" that confuses the clarity of Jesus' claim with the univocity of one conceptual system and one societal form. Repeatedly and unequivocally, von Balthasar stated his position against the temptation of integralism (for the last time in "Integralismus heute", *Diakonia* 19, 1988, pp. 221–29).

Although von Balthasar strongly emphasizes the utterly unique character of the form of Christ—as something which cannot be missed, or mistaken for anything else—and the unambiguity of his call, he also makes it clear that God's word demands a *free* response. This is the theme of the great trilogy: God's "showing of himself, giving of himself, uttering of himself" to human freedom. The beauty, the goodness and the truth of God, in their infinity and absoluteness, do not overwhelm or coerce the human person, but offer themselves to human freedom, which is itself created by God and always sustained by him: and they offer themselves as a free gift. God does not need coercion in order to prove that he is Lord. He has chosen the path of renunciation, in order to appeal to our freedom, to move it and to attract it. The form of his revelation, the crucified Christ, does not need to disclose its power in order to convince. It is sufficiently full of light in order to be clear, it bears its evidential character in itself.

This is why the Church needs no bastions in order to be the "city set on a hill". Her form of existence is most intelligible when it is like his form of existence. The permanently valid concern of *Razing the Bastions* is to demonstrate *this*: "See, I send you out like sheep among the wolves" (Mt 10:16). This is why von Balthasar points to holiness, which can be persecuted but not refuted (pp. 23–27). The Church is not allowed to howl along with the wolves in order to win sheep for the Lord. She is credible when her openness to the world does not become assimilation to the world—which would have nothing else to say to the world than what the world itself already knows better. She must remain "alien to the world", if she is to bear witness to what the world lacks. But it is precisely by being different in this way that she can show her deepest unity with the world—the new solidarity of which *Razing the Bastions* speaks and which takes its measure in Christ: "He is dead so that we may live, his light is extinguished so that the darkness in us may become bright" (p. 63). If the Church is "the consort who helps" Christ, "must not something of Christ's mystery be repeated in her too?" (p. 63).

Fr. Christoph Schönborn, O.P.

Fribourg
Feast of the Exaltation of the Cross
1988

I

DEPARTURE

The present era of the Church's "restoration" cannot deceive us about the extent of the crisis in
which the Church also is caught in league with the
world. The period of the newly established cadres
and forms may be short; immediately behind them,
the naked will to destroy sneers at all these things.
But the world that lies in the pangs of birth is a
humanity becoming aware for the first time of its
unity on this planet and of the duty of stewarding
itself, and it pursues these goals with a hitherto
unknown spiritual exertion. As far as its will and
consciousness are concerned, the cataclysms
through which it passes are cataclysms bursting
open membranes that had become too constrict-
ing; they are mighty expansions of horizons, from
a European (or an Asian) format to a world format.
The Church cannot avoid joining humanity in
ascertaining this cosmic situation and task, and in
accepting it. As Catholic Church, she is predes-
tined for this; in many aspects, she is prepared for
this (for example, in the will to engage in world
mission and to take hold of the appropriate instru-
ments for this), but in other aspects she finds herself taken by surprise and insufficiently equipped.

Perhaps she continued all too long after the Reformation to hand on the old intellectual framework
of the middle ages in her Counter-Reformation;
we recognize this in the scant help we receive if
we turn to Baroque theology in our need: its relationship to its own past leaps to the eye, but not its
relationship to its future. The nineteenth century
brought not only the external discovery of lands
and epochs but also the inner enrichment of history, and above all the immense wealth of Asia's
modes of thought; paleontology widened the horizons still more, enlarging them immeasurably. But
most of the Church's representatives remained
immersed in their own tradition, vigorously restor-
ing it once again at the end of the century, uncon-
cerned with the expanded field of view.

In young people—who in any case prepare
themselves for transformations, for catastrophes or
unheard-of expansions, and are willing to play
their part in bringing these about—the Church's
sidelines-position and self-preoccupation have
aroused a feeling of discomfort; indeed, this
ancient Church which, out of its vast storehouse of
the wisdom born of old age, continues to teach
and admonish, evokes in the young a sense of
unreality. Especially in the countries that experienced the World Wars and the intellectual collapse
of beloved and trusted traditions, that which is traditional is suspect not primarily because of its content, but by the very fact of its form, by the fact

that it represents something that has existed in the past. The language of young people changes quickly, becomes rough and "basic"; impatience is written on their brow, they want only to be a springboard for what is to come, and they are open and ready for this.

The official representatives of the Church, however, have immersed themselves in lengthy studies in their tradition, they have learned its cautious language and assimilated its cultivated mode of thought, and so they are familiar with the values of the traditional as a whole, particularly as Catholicism uses the word "tradition" to mean something else as well: the handing-on of Christian revelation through oral tradition. And since the theological determination of what may have been entrusted to the Church as revelation, outside of Scripture, is complicated, disputed and difficult to grasp (especially for laypeople), the laity will always be inclined to equate or confuse the theological principle of tradition with a more general Catholic preference for handing on what already exists.

This confusion affects all the forms—spiritual and worldly, liturgical, political and social—that have been carried along in the great river of history as its detritus, from late antiquity into the nineteenth and twentieth centuries: from Greek philosophy, the Constantinian order of state and Church, the realm of Charlemagne; from classical, medieval and humanist education, up to the

French Revolution and beyond. But all of this meets the eye of the approaching age as something bracketed off—not only as all historical being that has its time and has had it, and then, belonging to the past, can no longer make any straightforward claim of belonging to the future, but still more as a period that is withdrawing from us, closing itself, a period it is now possible to see thanks to its increasing distance. It is like a tree which would, at the end, condense itself into a seed once more, so as to enter the future in a quite new metamorphosis. Thus Europe (dissolved as a reality) closes in upon itself, in order to become the spirit and the idea (*Geist-idee*) of future humanity as a whole. Members of the young generation—at least, the best among them—are not particularly inclined to iconoclasm; they are familiar with a *pietas* (even if a rather distracted *pietas*), all the more so because little that is essential seems to them deserving of a place in the wide open framework of the future. The seriousness with which they often poke around in the past and put things to the test has often a strange character of resignation and identifies them as an intermediary generation between a future that is not yet here and a past that no longer directly concerns them and is already far removed. They occupy themselves with it almost as a way of passing the time, until finally someone is willing to give them a job, perhaps as late as the eleventh hour. For so much has been experienced, and almost more has been written down, and the Church was woven into all this like an omnipresent pattern.

Although only one motif, she has given the whole tapestry its character; all the contrary motifs and flanking motifs, including the most worldly mockers and antichrists, including even communists and nihilists, were determined by her presence, her strength and weakness, her position and negation. Empires and their philosophies decayed and became something belonging to the past, but the Church is still here and present, hung about with all these things of the past which extend into the present almost entirely thanks to her. Who would otherwise be concerned about the Greeks' doctrine of nature, about Henry IV's penitential path to Canossa, or Galileo's fate? The one partner alive and involved in the dialogue and struggle at that time lives like an Ahasuerus before us and is glad to relate what it experienced centuries ago.

This gives the Church a prestige and weight that come from her old age: no one in today's West is older than the Church. Let us say nothing for the moment about the most striking mark of her age: the fact that Christianity has dissolved in the course of the centuries like a crumbling rock into ever more churches, sects and confessions. All of these draw nourishment from the power of her unity and call her into question more than everything else, denying her in the fact of a world that is effectively striving toward her unity. Thus they display a deterioration process of the greatest magnitude (like the deterioration process, incidentally, of all the world religions which have divided themselves and dissolved in a similar manner).

No, we are oppressed by the very paradox that someone here knows so much at all (whereas we others know so little of the present and the future), and that this great knowledge which the One offers us is almost entirely knowledge of the past. . . . In the periods marked off by the brackets (from Constantine to the French Revolution), even the most worldly persons were impressed that the Church knew so much. Now, as the bracket closes, this impressiveness is no longer guaranteed; and we are compelled to ask: How will the Church manage not to remain within the slowly-narrowing pincers?

There are two means of retaining or renewing the vitality of a historical construction for the present and the future. The first is violent and comes from outside: namely, the destruction of the tradition, of the monuments and libraries, the archives and administrative bodies, perhaps the dissolution of the historical memory for generations, and consequently the necessity to begin afresh with a tabula rasa. The second is intellectual and comes from within: namely, the power of transcending; this is the vitality that is the lifeblood of all traditions, the vitality that knows the past and yet is able to separate itself from the past to the extent that this is required by responsibility and readiness for the future. Both means can be grace: the second, a radiant grace, the first, a harsh grace. It may be the case that, where the second is not effective, Providence must apply the first: bombs or even persecution. Extremists within the walls do not shrink from praying ardently that the Church may experience this. But it is not our duty nor is it the Christian way to pray in such a fashion and to invoke lightning from heaven upon the old house. (What we know of a Carmel is something different: the case in which a community prays that the bombs may hit it, so that the people in the surrounding area may be spared; this prayer was heard.) Thus there remains the second, demanding, difficult path: that of transcendence from within. In contrast to the spiritually explosive power of bombs (which experience has taught us not to overestimate), this second way contributes the spiritually explosive power of holiness, which is always something more than the wisdom of the tradition: it is the presence of the Holy Spirit for us in today's age.

As soon as holiness appears on the scene, anxiety and wrangling fall silent, even if the opposition (especially on the part of the tradition) does not. One can fight against holiness and perhaps, to all appearances, kill it. But one cannot refute it. One can fight against it and kill it, and this has always been done by a tradition closed in upon itself and attributing an absolute significance to itself. Perhaps holiness in visibly radiant missions is bestowed on the Church only so that the burning struggle between holiness and tradition may plainly demonstrate that tradition, unknown to itself, has slipped out of the living center of holiness. One need not reach for the case of a Joan of Arc; the case of Newman suffices: the case of Paul that is repeated throughout the centuries—"our beloved brother Paul with the wisdom that is his own", but whose writings are so "difficult to understand" in Peter's judgment, and "are twisted by people without education and firmness of character" (2 Pet 3:16); the case of John is sufficient: oppressed by an ambitious man, he sees himself thrust to the margin of the Church along with his brothers who "are not received" (3 Jn 9–10).

There exists in the Church no holiness that is excused from proving itself by means of opposition from the forces of inertia within the Church; in the confrontation with the new messengers of God, the long-established believer seems already *in possessione*: Is he not equipped with all that is useful? What need does he have of new prophets? The apostles laugh at the "tall tales of the women", telling of apparitions (Lk 24:11), before they themselves hasten to the tomb; the crowd laughs at the Pentecostal spirit of the apostles and thinks the apostles are drunk, even so early in the morning

(Acts 2:13); the wise philosophers and theologians of Athens turn up their noses at Paul's proclamation of the Resurrection (Acts 17:32). In fact, if it were not necessary to break through the hard shells of the *possidentes* again and again, how else would we have the proof of the power of this youthful holiness?

Through its opposition we see that tradition is continually in danger of becoming "Old Testament" and pharisaic; the ever-new gift of holiness to the Church is the mildest judgment God can send down upon his Bride. *See what you are doing to me*, says the Bridegroom to her. *I will show it to you in the fate you are preparing for those who are my most beloved. But just as they kiss the hand that strikes them, so I, your judge, remain betrothed to you in love. Strike—you hit only love!* Thus, one can fight against holiness, one can forbid it a certain external activity, but one cannot refute it. It is simply the greater power, and always a power of intellectual conviction and demonstration too. Quite clearly, holiness is the best proof that the Church still has something, indeed everything, to say to the present and the coming time, *despite* her age and her wisdom of old age.

Thus one must look clearly at the point where this youthful holiness breaks through the shell of what has been, emerging into the light of the world now, fresh as on the first day. It may be difficult to observe this point because the holiness that is canonized (and today in greater numbers than ever before) has already, if not long ago, become history and tradition—indeed, in certain circumstances, itself a process belonging to the forces of tradition, and reinforcing them.

With its unconcern for the stockpiling of wisdom, holiness tends to break through at a distance from the established centers of tradition, and with a kind of indifference to them, and this too impedes our observation of its breakthrough point. It is with a certain naïveté that today's worker priests go among the poorest of the poor, and certainly not with the intention of reading with them Augustine or John of Saint Thomas. This naïveté—only the most visible element in all the freshness and clear-sightedness of the saint in today's Church, *one* point among others—ought not to give the appearance of creating a gulf between the life of today and the historical tradition. For a holy theologian could appear with that same power of persuasion, one who would bring the holy audacity of the worker priests to the plane of meditation and doctrine. No one can say in advance how his theology would look. But it is certain that supernatural force of *life* could work just as mightily in the realm of the intellect as the supernatural power of *spirit* now works through the worker priests on the plane of immediate life. What many of them display in their life is a genuine spirit of the Gospel, rising up like a spring of water from their immediate relationship to Christ, unweakened in the least by temporal and historical distance.

Holiness is always the refutation of the idea that time plays an essential role in Christianity; strangely enough, the reverse is true: our temporal distance allows us to come more directly to the source: namely, to the revelation of Christ. In a glance we perceive that all that has been realized hitherto is not what Christ now, immediately demands of me, of you, of our generation; that history knows no solution for this hour (for the simple reason that it is history, and not the present day); and since history does not know, we are free to look at the Gospel and its simple solution. But the lengthy and laborious experiences of centuries past are not superfluous when this leap into the Gospel is taken; the account of them shows us where certain paths lead, how far one comes away from the origins in certain circumstances, how powerful or weak the solutions are, how transient and time-conditioned are the syntheses between revelation and culture, and how inappropriate to the total grace and mission of the Gospel are the translations thought out by men.

There are indeed theologians who appear to think that theology (that is, the exposition of revelation in human concepts) has progressed so far that it stands virtually before its conclusion. The house seems to be built and the walls already papered; a smaller and more subtle work remains for each coming generation: the decoration of the finished rooms and of the spaces (becoming smaller all the time) between these rooms, and keeping order in the drawers. In the end, only the dusting will remain. Such a view is the result of looking only at the tradition. But when the saint (or indeed, anyone who believes and who receives grace in a living manner) compares the tradition with the immensities of revelation itself, does not all that has been attained collapse into a miserable little heap of thoughts and concepts, scarcely the ABC of revelation? *Si comprehendis, non est Deus*; Augustine repeated this a hundred times. In reality, even—and precisely—the theologian who has intensively studied the endeavors of the learned divines will be overwhelmingly aware, when he contemplates revelation, that *as yet almost nothing has been done*, that immense areas remain to be investigated, whole continents on this map remain white spaces.

Our concern is not to run down, pick apart and make light of what has been produced in earlier ages: all that is genuinely true remains. But sketches are not yet a fully-executed painting. And many such sketches, drawn up in the third and fourth centuries, remain almost unchanged to the present day, as if they already were the painting. Let us ask only about the most elementary matters. The three center-points of a Christian theology are beyond doubt the doctrine of the triune God, of God the Word made manifest in the flesh in Christ, and of God the Spirit who expounds the revelation of love in the Church and in her members. What place does the doctrine about the triune God have in Christian existence? And what place has it had in theology, in which this doctrine seems to have stood still, half-congealed and dried up after Augustine's psychological speculation?

There would be so many other paths besides that of Augustine, perhaps ever better paths (for ultimately, the solitary structure of the soul cannot supply the supreme image for the living exchange of love in the eternal God). Why does no one seek these paths and follow them out? Christian proclamation in the school, from the pulpit, and in the lecture halls of the universities could be so much more alive, if *all* the theological tractates were given a completely trinitarian form! And what a dryness there is in the doctrine about Christ, which likewise has made scarcely any progress since Chalcedon, where an abstract formula has to answer for the central mystery. Once again the formula is excellent, but only if it is a skeletal structure that enables the living flesh of the word of revelation to stand and to walk.

A theological interpretation of the whole Gospel in terms of christology has never been made, however. Theology circles around the abstract and somehow timeless fundamental formulas, and spirituality considers the events of the life of Jesus and of salvation history in their totality: their betrothal has not taken place—and so much fruitfulness could be expected of this betrothal. And this has been the case, not least because the "spiritual exposition" of Scripture, grounded thoroughly and correctly by the Church Fathers despite many mistakes and insufficient technical equipment, was more and more neglected later on and is as good as forgotten today.[1] What is the theology of Cana? Or of the walking on the water? Or of the burial? Or of the resurrection appearances? Or, to move to an adjacent area: What is the ecclesiology, the theology of the Acts of the Apostles? The theology of Peter and John, of Paul and James? Not the theology of their "teaching", but of their existence, their person and history?

Of course, in order to have the most basic understanding of this question (although, seen in Christian terms, it is an elementary question), one must first have grasped that theology is the doctrine of the divine meaning of the revelation of the historical events of revelation themselves—nothing above them, nothing behind them, nothing that one could take away and retain as a suprahistorical substance—and that therefore, the more the historical discloses itself in a theological sense, the more does theology develop. Similarly, the changed his-

[1] See Henri de Lubac, *Histoire et esprit: l'Intelligence de l'Ecriture* (Paris: Aubier-Montaigne, 1950), chap. 4.

torical situation offers the theology of the Church new access-roads which lead unexpectedly into the deepest areas. It was not only the undeveloped concept of history that prevented a development of ecclesiology during the middle ages but also the position of the Church vis-à-vis the world surrounding her at that time. She had a very summary relationship to the non-Christian world—pagans, Jews, heretics, schismatics—even as late as the period of the missionary mendicant Orders. At the level of consciousness humanity possessed at that period, an awareness of ultimate solidarity and fellowship in destiny could not yet exist, and one cannot presuppose such an awareness without anachronism; this is why very profound questions of ecclesiology and of such Church-related areas as protology (predestination) and eschatology remain unanswered.

Whole centuries felt no need to think about precisely those questions which agitate us most today; to a large extent they could be content with an "image", an "idea", where we must struggle at all costs to achieve the reflection of the image in a genuine concept. The time is ripe to pose questions that the few generations separating us from Christ had not found the time yet to see and think about. If things were otherwise, where would the Holy Spirit remain in history? According to Christ's promise, he will lead us into all the truth. He will do this until the end of the world, and without repeating himself. He will illuminate new depths of revelation from century to century, depths that earlier times had indeed "seen" yet without paying attention to them, just as one can pass a house every day for years without once looking at it properly.

Thus, Francis of Assisi was a new light on the Gospel; perhaps, as the distance increases, he will be understood more and more as the summit of the middle ages in his relationship to revelation. The true peaks rise as the distance grows; we must take care not to consider our own age as an age without salvation or saints. Everything depends on the awareness that we have of our Christianity. For Francis, to be a Christian was something just as immense, certain and startlingly glorious as to be a human being, a youth, a man. And because being a Christian is eternal being and eternal youth, without danger of withering and resignation, his immediate joy was deeper. Not one single year separated him from Christ, the one who had become flesh; from the manger; from the Cross. For him, not one speck of dust had settled on the freshness of the wonder in the passage of time. The *hodie* of the liturgy on the great feasts was the *hodie* of his life. Is there a saint who has had any other Christian consciousness of time?

Those then who take up the burden of two thousand years of ecclesiastical tradition, in order to bring the full light to bear, first upon themselves and then, from themselves, upon the present day, must do so with the same youthfulness inherent in their being Christian: every formula that is discovered must be transparent to the event both of then and of today; it is to be made use of to the extent that it permits what was then to become reality today, and left unused to the extent that it impedes this. In the many complicated systems of thought, perhaps only one thing remains vital today: namely, that in them we can discover what other ages knew about encountering the overwhelming mystery of God. Where this can no longer be discerned, the systems quite deserve to be utterly forgotten. (A truth that was not alive, or that could not be made alive once more, would certainly be no truth.) In the framework of Christian living and thinking, tradition can be nothing else than allowing oneself to be carried by the spiritual power of earlier generations, so that one may oneself, alive, come closer to the mystery. Thus one can adopt not only the correctness of findings and formulas but also—unconditionally, and as the more important element in the truth—the immediate relationship to the event.

The truth of Christian life is like manna: it is not possible to hoard it for it is fresh today and spoiled tomorrow. A truth that is merely handed on, without being thought anew from its very foundations, has lost its vital power. The vessel that holds it— for example, the language, the world of images and concepts—becomes dusty, rusts, crumbles away; that which is old remains young only when it is drawn, with all the strength of youth, into relation with that which is still older, with that in time which is perpetual: the present-day revelation of God. No Holy Communion is like another, although it is the same Christ who gives himself. In the same way, no sermon and no word of doctrine, indeed no Christian word at all and no Christian thought can be the same as any other, although each is a vessel and a form of the one, eternal Word among us. To honor the tradition does not excuse one from the obligation of beginning everything from the beginning each time, not with Augustine or Thomas or Newman, but with Christ. And the greatest figures of Christian salvation history are honored only by the one who does today what they did then, or what they would have done if they had lived today. The cross-check is quickly done, and it shows the tremendous impoverishment, not only in spirit and life, but also quite existentially: in thoughts and points of view, themes and ideas, where people are content to understand tradition as the handing-on of ready-made results. Boredom manifests itself at once, and the neatest systematics fails to convince, remains of little consequence. The little groups of those who have come to an understanding with one another and cultivate what they take to be the tradition become more and more esoteric, foreign to the

world, and more and more misunderstood, although they do not condescend to take notice of
their alienation. And one day the storm that blows
the dried-up branch away can no longer be
delayed, and this collapse will not be great, because
what collapses had been a hollow shell for a very
long time.

But where the Spirit moves vitally in the Body a
continuous, unwearying process of becoming new
is under way, although the identity of the Person
(the mystical Christ) is always the same. The
supra-temporality of Catholic truth is not an atem-
porality, for Christ has become a human being and
has grown from embryo to man, and he continues
to grow in his members as they come into being,
and in the forms that his Church takes through the
ages. The "last times" are not the end of time, but
the consequence of the fullness of the times. Old
Covenant revelation grew toward this fullness
amid lightning and thunder in an unceasing stream
of events; thus the Jews could construct no theology or tradition other than one whose essential
point was the laying open of all that had happened
in the past to the unforeseeable event of the coming of God in the future. Even where the increasing light of revelation fell backward onto salvation
history and opened up for meditation the deliverance from Egypt, the Covenant on Sinai, the entry
into the promised land, the interpretation of history always received its whole power from the

consciousness that the individual and the nation had of the present, and this was as such a consciousness of the future: an awareness of itself as the bearer of a coming history, pregnant with a fruit that Mary yearns for and prays for even in the ninth month, but a fruit inconceivable in its outward appearance, its destiny and the demands it would make, witness in advance of the God who is in every case greater. And when God came in the fullness of time and fulfilled everything, he was not the end of revelation but its beginning: everything had begun from the beginning of the world in view of this beginning. *En archē ēn ho Logos*: What else should the Logos bring but the beginning?

Revelation is "closed" (with the death of the last apostle) only because the infinite fullness can no longer grow, but it can radiate forth its fullness into infinity, and under its sun everything can grow to full maturity. And if conclusions seemed possible everywhere in the Old Covenant (since it was letter), then openings, beginnings and the inchoate must show themselves everywhere in the New Covenant, since it is spirit. Every truth is now explosive: it divides itself into thousands of truths, each one of which has the force of the starting point. In the case of Paul and John, one can observe this characteristic of the New Testament truth directly, but it is also revealed in the immense dynamism lying *behind* the words of an

Irenaeus, a Clement, Basil, Augustine, Thomas
Aquinas, Pascal, Bernanos. Those who study their
clarity and logic are themselves caught up into the
whirlwind of the Holy Spirit by this same force.
Where he was not to be felt, there could be no
testimony to the truth of Christ. The Spirit wishes
to lead us into all truth, but it is not his way to deal
out careful doses of "all truth", dispensing only
"some truth" each time, perhaps in slowly increasing doses easier for men to tolerate. Ever since the
whirlwind of Easter and Pentecost, the superabundance of *all* truth is always on the scene, and neither an ecclesiastical nor an intellectual (*geistige*)
order (which likewise derives from the Holy Spirit
[*Geist*]) will ever have this superabundance under
its control, or ever be anything other than the vessel in which this effervescence is served to us.

And so there sounds forth to all Christian generations the same radiant "*Fanget an!* Begin!" of *Die
Meistersinger*. For its part, this rejuvenating time
comes upon them in a way different from the
Holy Spirit's, and confronts them with a situation
that is young. Both, the Spirit and the time,
awaken them from the bed of historical sleep for
the deed of today. This deed will witness to Christ
through a Church that has interpreted, understood
and responded to the signs of the times, above all
by understanding how to move and to make use of
herself and her own structures, like living limbs, in
a new and different way.

The limbs of a man are limited in number and determined in function, yet no individual makes full use of every potential with which his limbs are endowed and for which they can be trained. The structure of the Church—likewise a clear, determined and unchangeable structure in its fundamental articulations—proves much more flexible in the course of her history, because she belongs more to the realm of the spirit; her sinews, ligaments and joints, of which Paul speaks, can play a much subtler game through the ages. The fundamental structure itself can be interpreted by the Spirit in ever new ways, illuminated and made use of by him. In the middle ages, it seemed that the structure assimilated itself totally to the worldly system of ordered states in an intentional mimicry (such that people began to speak of ecclesiastical classes), and the Petrine-hierarchical element reflected, in the realm of the spirit, the Constantinian-Carolingian hierarchy.

Today there is no doubt that the hour of the laity is sounding in the Church. Previously, despite the emperor and the sacramental of his anointing, despite the Templars and the Knights of St. John, the laity counted for little. The theology of this was made by priests and the result accorded with that fact. The church buildings of that time (such a heavy burden for our acts of worship today, since it is impossible or very difficult to realize the liturgy in them as a community celebration) at best

allowed only the lay elite into the most sacred pre-
cincts, while the people had to remain at the back.
Neither Gert Groote's movement nor that of Francis de Sales was taken up by the general consciousness of the Church in their day; on the contrary,
after the exit of the protesters in rage, Baroque
theology once again stressed distance-creating elements.

Today, a sleeping giant is stretching himself;
undreamt-of powers, lying idle up to now like the
powers in water not yet brought together to form
a dam, and pregnant with primal energies, are
beginning to move. Catholic Action has sum-
moned the giant, and in the lay institutes of today
and in a thousand individual undertakings we see
that the call was heard and that the layman is
beginning to take up the responsibility that is his
own. The powers are so great that we must see the
simultaneous emphasis of organization and centralization in today's Church as a grace of Providence,
designed to order those energies so that they do
not waste themselves in bluster. But organization
and centralization are living values only when the
strong energies fill the turbines and drive them
round.

Here we see also the meaning of the Mariology,
surprising to many, that suddenly comes into
prominence in a seemingly one-sided way, devel-
oping like a hypertrophied twig on the tree of the
Church's teaching, twig by twig; now, the eccle-

sial meaning of the Marian dogmas reveals itself:
Mary is the womb and archetype of the Church,
she is the fruitfulness of the Church herself, she is
the internal form of the Church, since she is the
Bride of Christ. Mary stands closer to Christ than
Peter and than the other apostles: where Peter
embodies the official ministry of the Church, Mary
incorporates the totality of the Church; where
Peter is the one who administers, Mary is the one
who says "yes", who is herself administered and
taken by the Bridegroom; where Peter must
demand obedience, Mary is the virginal-nuptial
vessel of all obedience, out of which flows not
only the Christian's obedience but Peter's demands
as well. The opposition between Peter and his
flock, between the hierarchy and the laity, is
superseded in Mary and taken into the deeper reality that is the basis of both: into the reality of the
Church as Bride. And the idea of obedience too,
which the last of the great ecclesial Orders, standing with one foot in the medieval order of social
classes, has fully developed, takes on an undreamt-
of deepening in the fundamental Marian attitude of
the Church and of each individual in the Church;
only now has this Marian grounding become
something conscious. In her presentation of herself, the Petrine Church has come upon what lies
deeper in her own being, without which this
being would be merely a monster: obedience in
the Church is nothing other than love, the form

and fruitfulness of bridal love. And thus the juridi-
cal-moral concept of merit, in use till now, is irre-
sistibly giving way—in keeping with revelation—
to the deeper, universal concept of fruit.

But with Mary, John too must come forward in
the Church. He takes his place at a strangely veiled
midpoint exposed to all winds, between Peter, to
whom he is united by mission and apostolate, and
Mary, to whom he is united both by the commission to love given under the Cross and by that
pure love to the Lord that is not to be exhausted in
any one form. With one hand in Peter's and the
other in Mary's, he unites Mary to Peter in terms
of their mission. (This does not prevent Mary, as
Ekklēsia, from being the higher midpoint between
both apostles, nor Peter from remaining the visible
midpoint as the one who administers everything,
including love, including Mary.) The Mariology
which has been brought into prominence will
slowly prepare the way for a future ecclesiology
(though perhaps it can never be so exoterically formulated as the dogmas of Mary's individual privileges can be); more important, it will furnish the
basis for the new ecclesial consciousness, especially
that of the laity.

The intellectual situation of the Church has perhaps never been so open, so full of promise and so
pregnant with the future at any time since the first
three centuries. When Christians today take a
pause on their pilgrimage and look back at the

road they have covered, they see the horizons retreating and closing to form images that can be taken in at one glance; and, as the poet says, one can take leave of them with a blessing, rather than with a broken heart. The doors stand open for every new commitment, every initiative, especially on the part of laymen. And they ought seriously to tell themselves that the increased activity in the Church's organizational centers is often traceable not simply to the good will of the occupants but just as often to the lack of participation and imagination both intellectual and spiritual on the part of the lay groups. Where much ought to be in movement but only a little is in movement, one need not be surprised if an attempt is made to muzzle people. And those who are merely onlookers and do not themselves take part are those least entitled to criticize.

The future of the Church (and today she has the greatest opportunities) depends on whether laymen can be found who live out of the unbroken power of the Gospel and are willing to shape the world. It is obvious to everyone who sees clearly that the clergy and the Orders *can* no longer suffice for this. They are not at fault; rather, the cause lies in the irresistible process whereby the world has been maturing since the middle ages, with an ever clearer distinction between the *civitas terrena* and the *civitas Dei* (such as we find sanctioned in the definitions of the First Vatican Council, for example). Wherever the world-clock has struck this hour, the emergence of a new form of Christian apostolate is a foregone conclusion. And all that counts is to hear the voice of Christ as he makes election, and to make oneself available with the same joyfulness once shown by the apostles. Certainly, two figures, visible to all, have risen up in today's Church: the worker priest and the consecrated layman (Opus Dei, for example). And in both cases, the privileged classes have descended from the throne of their privileges: the class of priests has descended into the class of the laity, so that—at least outwardly—they can be absorbed into it without distinctions; and the class of the Orders has descended into the class of those who live in the world, so that the simple Christian among other Christians may do what all have to do on earth: live and work for the salvation of the world in the world. Not everyone is called to the same thing, but everyone is called to recognize and further these radiant signs of the times.

What must at all costs be shattered is the historical consciousness of Christians, a consciousness which has become senile because the pulse that beats in it is a pulse of insufficient faith. Signs of age, indeed signs of decay (like the Reformation and all its consequences), appear on the body of the Church. But already Augustine and Gregory the Great saw the Church as covered with such abscesses, and concluded that the last times had come. From the perspective of the philosophy of history, the Church is superannuated; she has been here far too long and has been superseded. And since the Church is *also* an entity in world history, it should certainly be possible to observe signs in her organism that she has outlived herself in this way.

In terms of the history of religion, each year the Church spends on earth is another proof she will the sooner die; no religion on earth lives much longer than two thousand years. And seen psychologically, it is impossible, even in an individual, for a consciousness burdened with so much (and ever-increasing) tradition to maintain the freshness and carefreeness of the first youthful Christianity. Who could cope adequately even with what is already at hand? (And yet this is something incomparably more important to Catholics and more incumbent upon them than it is other Christians.) And then who has reserved still enough strength besides to grasp clearly today's mission for the Church of today's times, and to tackle this mission without succumbing to exhaustion? Does not experience show that the personalities capable of managing both tasks are sown so thinly that one can only consider them exceptions, and those who first must get a grip on history, in order then to be equipped for working in our time, mostly do not get a grip on history, and remain handicapped?

These are all questions drawn from harsh reality; nevertheless, they are all assessments made by unbelief; they are all heavy stones rolled in front of the tomb, yet they cannot stop the daily miracle of the resurrection. Once again: if the burden of the Old Testament letter was not too heavy to be transformed into spirit, how then should the burden of the New Testament letter—already spirit in its internal dimension—be too heavy for the one who has received all power in heaven and on earth? The Church and the Christians in her do not fit any categories of the histories of philosophy, psychology or sociology such that they could be definitively described on the basis of these categories. A Christian transcends these laws precisely to the extent that he believes. He does not owe it to the flesh to live according to the flesh, nor does he owe it to the laws of historical sociology to conform to them. But can it not be observed that at least the majority, the mass in the Church obeys these laws, precisely because their awareness of history has fallen asleep? And the consequence is the great defections which in turn, as new "failures", introduce new uncertainty among the masses, bringing in their train, in a vicious circle, yet more defections.

Nevertheless, one must reply that the "mass" was just as problematical in Cyprian's and Augustine's times as it is today: the persecutions removed this stubble but better times brought it back. During the floods of the Reformation, masses like this floated off without really noticing it (Sweden, for example), and thus remained outside by chance. Everything depends on the Twelve and on those who, from their hands, have inherited the light: the faith, not in success but in the inexhaustible power of the charge which has been given. Success, said Martin Buber, is not one of the names of God. But one of his names is consuming fire, and the Son came to cast this fire upon the earth. Is it possible that in today's drought that fire should no longer have anything to consume?

II

DESCENT

The fact that history passes like a wandering ray of sunlight over the statue of unchangeable truth gives this statue life and tension. Or should one say that the truth, even the truth that endures, ought not at all to be compared to rigid stone, but itself possesses a fullness of interior life that can present itself ever anew without denying the past? The truth of the Church is always the same, but the onward march of the world's hour puts it into a new light, into altered relationships that allow something new, something altered, to become visible in the truth itself. The tension and drama of its existence in the world and of its relationship to the world around it increase with each century.

Two great changes have occurred in this relationship since the middle ages, two turning-points: within Christianity, the Western division of the Church with its consequences for ecclesial consciousness, and, closely connected to this, an altered awareness of the non-Christian world. For the medieval Christian, Christianity and the civilized world are one. Only Byzantium is a sizable, broken-off fragment on the margin; the other schismatic Eastern Churches scarcely count. And whatever stands in opposition to the unity in the Western area is always quickly (and usually with political measures of force) reabsorbed into the unity. This means that the boundaries *ad extra* are sharply drawn for consciousness too; Christianity is a fortified *civitas*, whose fortified outposts—above all in the direction of the Crescent Moon—are defended by stalwart warriors of the Church: Granada, Marienburg, Rhodes. . . . The Church's awareness was limited by these political and geographical boundaries in a way scarcely possible for us to grasp today. The Christian thought in a closed inner room, his Christian awareness emerged only weakly and vaguely *ad extra* over the boundaries. At most, he is vitally concerned with pushing the boundaries forward, with winning new territory (wrested in war from unfruitful paganism and made accessible to the fruitful cultivation, *cultura*, of the Church); he is occupied with the Crusades, the physical weakening of pagan strength, the retaking of the Holy Land within the sheltering walls of the *civitas*; at best, he is occupied with that intellectual war in which the *spolia Aegyptiorum*—the worldly wisdom of Plato, Aristotle and Plotinus, unjustly held captive among pagans, Jews and Muslims—is to be brought back home to that authentic domain wherein all truth is stewarded: the Church and her theology.

From the fifteenth century onward, this changes. The discovery of unknown continents brings humanity together into a unity that can be seen in its totality; the defending walls of the old cities and fortresses slowly give way, uniting the closed inner spaces with the countryside. Both the geographical-political inner room and the spiritual-intellectual inner room of Christianity find themselves unexpectedly brought into a continuity with the surrounding world, and this situation demanded (and still demands) that all the instincts be newly attuned and the interior organs of balance differently disposed. The demand was all the harsher in that the sense of inner security was also cruelly disturbed from the outside now: the rending of Western Church unity, deepening ever further, with a generative power revealed in the ever quicker divisions of the Protestant churches. At one blow this rending struck from the Christian's hand both the external weapons and the strongest internal weapons. For it could not be denied that the division of the Western Church was evident proof for the former outsiders—Jews, Muslims and pagans—of the decisive defeat, the fatal weakening of the alleged *civitas Dei*: and this not merely in the superficial sense that it would be easy to strike a foe who is busy attacking himself, but in the deeper sense that Christianity denied its own obedience of faith to the commandment of Christ, abandoning this obedience.

Christians were meant to be one "as the Father and I are one", but they were not one; they were meant to love one another, that the world would recognize the truth of the new teaching, but they did not love one another. Through the division of faith, Christianity had refuted itself. Moreover, the separated ice-floes began to be driven ever faster and farther away from one another on the waves of history, and each one initiated a powerful development of its own which was also conditioned by the negation of the opponent. The intellectual languages and forms of experience became alienated from one another, so that, humanly speaking, it was no longer possible at all to conceive of a reversion to unity.

The Catholic Church, until then the crown on a pyramid of orders and kingdoms all oriented toward herself, thus saw herself now doubly deposed: the collapse of the outer walls had brought her into a horizontal (and no longer a hierarchical) solidarity with the whole of humanity; the collapse within herself had rendered her, to all appearances, one church among other churches. And the many churches, the more they became small sects or mere structures of liberal religion on their margins, seemed to mediate a kind of seamless transition from the Catholic sphere to the most worldly sphere. Where earlier the one church spire had risen above the sea of roofs and dominated them without question, now other towers rise up, and as time passes it becomes increasingly difficult to determine whether these are spiritual or worldly towers: whether they are monuments of devotion (or symbols of power) that are "still" religious, or ones that are "long since" secular.

What is called the Counter-Reformation, strictly speaking, was still too dominated by the determination to carry on as long as possible the medieval order, for it to be able to encompass the elements needed for a real mastery of the new situation. The splendor of this salvage attempt has passed away,[1] with its authentic grandeur as well as its theater of appearances, and the world is the poorer for its passing; indeed, only now did the world become truly poor. The person who belongs to the Church today must attempt, painstakingly and gropingly in the presence of God, to interpret the plans of Providence for the Church in today's world, in this as yet unmastered situation.

The way ahead must lie in the intellectual domain: a path defined negatively by two solu-

[1] In order to come to know the spirit of Baroque theology, one should read not so much the commentators of Aquinas' *Summa*, who essentially do not lead beyond Thomas and his age, but rather the great actors and decorators with their stupendous breadth of knowledge: a Kircher, Caramuel von Lobkowitz, Théophile Raynaud. At the same time, one should look behind the stage-set to see the machinery of the presentation. Little can be found in these mighty quarries and curiosity shops: here and there a strange piece, but certainly no synthesis, and that which still remains of the endless moral tractates—between the Stoics and probabilism! Truly has it been truly observed: the Baroque had so much to form and to build that it had too little time left to think (theologically). Its achievement is immense; even today, it overwhelms the senses and the imagination. But we feel all the more the gap in the spirit, the lack of continuity, as this came to be felt subsequently in the nineteenth century.

tions, neither of which can be followed. The first is the solution of an absolutism of the truth, which does not understand the new situation of solidarity, but wishes to deal with the people of our time on the same level of consciousness that characterized medieval absolutism. The other is the religious relativism of the Enlightenment: the very understandable and initially unavoidable reaction to that absolutism and to the new situation created by mankind's discoveries in space and time, by the Reformation and the fall of barriers; this reaction now understands all forms of religion as meaningful, justified and complementary to one another on various levels of relationship to a total truth. Now, if the path between these two is to be the correct path, it cannot consist of a compromise between them. It must bring to the surface a truth and an attitude that, as Catholic truth and attitude, display to the world a clear, defined and unmistakable countenance. One must not be surprised that this new Catholic attitude is difficult to understand for the unbelieving world (and often too for the Christian who has not yet adapted to it); and that indeed it contains a mysterious audacity and an apparent paradox, in keeping with the lateness of the hour; and that ultimately it cannot be explained in a perfectly rational manner at all, because all that is Catholic shares in the mysterious character of divine revelation. On the contrary, all this is an aspect of the way things are.

Two reflections will make clear in what direction one must look. The first aims at a rethinking of the ancient axiom rigorously expounded by Augustine, "outside the Church there is no salvation". (The earlier Church Fathers, who had been the first to employ it, were less strict.) According to Augustine, there is hope of salvation for every man as long as he lives, that is to say, as long as he can repent of sin and, if he is outside the Catholic Church, can convert to her. This interpretation, certainly not the universal interpretation even in the middle ages, was from the outset wholly in accord with the vision of a visibly demarcated *civitas Dei* on earth: a supernatural realm of light over against which stands another region, equally clearly demarcated—one that could not be illuminated in all eternity.

When the Enlightenment and religious relativism rejected this dualism, they also threw overboard the above-mentioned axiom. Everyone is to be blessed in his own fashion; outside the Church there is every possibility of salvation. Now, it is of course true that the Church, combating the Jansenism which was a petrified remnant of the medieval strictness, had rejected the proposition that "there is no grace outside the Church"; and if there is grace, then surely there is also deliverance, and also salvation. There exists a baptism of desire, just as there is a Holy Communion of desire and a sacramental confession of desire, and a hidden supernatural life in the presence of God—and to say this is to say much more than is recognized in a Rousseauvian or Enlightenment notion of an uncorrupted nature. But what then is the point of the Church?

Only now does the genuine point begin to appear: the grace of Christ, which is universal, merited on the Cross for all, is not distributed without regard for the Bride, the Church. Head and Body are One Christ: Augustine himself had laid down this premise. Without Christ, there is no access to the Father. Without the Church, there is no participation in Christ. The Church is this participation, and consequently the mediation of this participation also. This has an internal aspect: the Catholic unity of the "treasury of grace"; here there is no longer any distinction between what is the grace of Christ and what is the grace of his saints, the highest of whom is the "mediatrix of all graces"—his Mother, the archetype and real symbol of his Bride. And it has an external aspect: the unity of the mediation of salvation to the world through the one, heavenly-invisible, and earthly-visible and hierarchical Church. "I am the light of the world"; "you are the light of the world": there is only the One light poured forth. "No salvation outside the Church" means then, in both an interior and an exterior sense, that no salvation is mediated except through the Church. The Church is the instrument of the mediation of salvation to the world, for she is the mystical Body of Christ, into which the Word of God descended for the sake of redemption.

This transformation of awareness in the theological realm would have been difficult to achieve without the secession of the Reformation and its consequences. We are far from wishing to give this terrible event of Christian guilt something like the stamp of a necessary and indeed happy event in the history of ideas; nevertheless, in the power of redemptive grace, God can make use of what is for us unforgivable sin to further his mysterious purposes. When finally the dreadful words *crepuit medius* could be uttered over a guilty Christendom, long eaten away at by the illness of the Great Schism, then it was necessary to take up the following words too: *et diffusa sunt omnia viscera ejus.*

Something of the innermost bowels of the Church had been torn out of the Church by the Reformers, something of her heart continued to beat outside her heart, in a transposition for which we have no metaphor. Not only are all the validly baptized outside the Catholic Church her children in truth, belonging to her by right and whom she misses bitterly because her breasts yearn for them and the pain of the milk that is not sucked torments her; there is much more than this: profound mysteries, things that often only her saints knew, were stolen from her by the Augustinian of Wittenberg and borne off by night from her treasure chamber. Now her goods lie on the open street, for that which calls itself "Church" outside her has no inner room, knows no mystery, is pulled to pieces in the lecture halls; everyone can take his piece of it and gather a new conventicle around it. (And Karl Barth may be correct to say the conventicles have often preserved more Christian vitality than the so-called churches.) In this way the love of the Church has been moved out of her, tragically and utterly irremediably, often still recognizable in the pieces of her lying about in front of her doors. But the more they become dissolved in the world, the more unrecognizable they become. Finally they will be concealed in the elements of the cosmos, like the chorus that dissolves itself at the end of the Helena-act, like a beloved tomb that one continues to visit for a long time although it has lain empty for years.

But the image is not valid, for what once was Church and supernature cannot return to world and nature—unless these latter were permeated by an invisible aura. What a strangely new meaning for the Bride Church take on those words, once the object of so much commentary, from the Song of Songs: *Curremus in odorem unguentorum tuorum*, now that the invisible fragrances of the Beloved are scattered in the most worldly parts of the world and suddenly accost the unperceiving Bride as she hastens through uncharted places after the invisible One.

O you lost god! You never-ending clue!
Only since hatred at last parceled you among us,
are we hearers and a mouth for nature.[2]

The collapse of the internal unity and the razing of the external bastions have thus not remained without consequences for the Church's consciousness: not only an essential principle about the unity of salvation and Church, but also an existential self-knowledge in the depths of the Church as subject has changed. The theologians seem to sense little of this, since they only rarely and in exceptional cases feel themselves challenged by the truth outside—for example, by what is true in Protestant dogmatics. But the Church as a whole senses more, and the extrapolated awareness effected through the *felix culpa* of the wounds inflicted has created an indissoluble solidarity with the separated brethren, and through them with the world. Now this awareness begins to move with the freshness of springtime among the responsible laity.

Through the mediation of those who have left, a new form of osmosis between Church and world is beginning, like a breath, drawing in and out. And because of the new responsibility for the inner realm which has now been "externalized", the bond to that which is genuinely external becomes ever more indissoluble: this external realm is now understood to be the world of all the brethren in

[2] Rilke, *Sonnets to Orpheus*, transl. C. F. MacIntyre (Berkeley: University of California Press, 1960), I, 26.

Christ, of all those who are genuinely waiting for grace and for the Word that is to be proclaimed to them.

The immense transformation in Christian consciousness that must come about on the basis of this insight is a transformation from possessor to giver, from usufructuary to apostle, from privileged person to responsible person. In the middle ages, and still in the Baroque period, the former attitude was the essential one; the latter followed as a possible derivative at best. Things could not be otherwise as long as the Augustinian view of predestination—two classes of men from the very outset, one chosen and the other rejected—was seriously taken as basic. One cannot say that the medieval Christian felt himself, fundamentally, and in his very identity as a Christian, responsible for the non-Christian. Such a feeling presupposes a new stage of Christian awareness, at which the *purpose* of election becomes clear. The medieval Christian's naïve, because wholly unreflective, egotism of salvation cannot be reproached; it would have to be censured today, however, now that the bastions have fallen and the element of solidarity makes its appearance for the first time in the awareness of a humanity united. (On this point, one can consult Bergson's *Deux Sources*.)

It is not that the Christian *too*—like all the others, and perhaps against his own will and as the last of all in the age of social awareness—begins to

think in terms that are a little more social than previously. Rather, because of the barriers that have
been pulled down, something has awakened in the
Church's consciousness that cannot be rooted and
related in the spirit of any other man: the knowledge that his election means being sent to those
who are not chosen, means vicarious representa-
tion, bearing responsibility, sacrifice. Objectively,
this was always the case; Anthony, going off into
the wilderness, was already then an apostle and the
light of the world. But what had not yet existed
subjectively now comes into being, when the great
Teresa establishes her Carmel for missionary reasons, as an aid of prayer in the Church and a con-
tribution to the Church's strength and the
Church's light in the darkness.

Augustine and the middle ages read and understood Romans, chapter nine, and they trembled
before the mystery. We read it too, but we find
the solution for what makes us tremble in chapters
ten and eleven, which the middle ages did not yet
perceive in their terribly extensive, exorbitantly
demanding, universal significance. The parable of
the two brothers, the one rejected and the other
chosen, becomes transparent in its reference to the
intended truth about the chosen and the rejected
people. But now these two stand alternately for
one another in a unique dialectic that cannot be
illuminated by any other example, a dialectic that
is the essence of the Christian theology of history:

the chosen people is rejected because of its guilt, so that the non-people which was not chosen may be brought into election; and in its turn this non-people is chosen so that the first promise to the chosen people may reach its fullness, so that Israel may become spiritual and as such, that is, as universal, as "Israel as a whole, may be saved". "For God's gifts of grace and his calling are irrevocable."

And so the exorbitant demand in the apostolic idea has a strange calming as its consequence: if the responsibility for my brother becomes an unbearably heavy load, the heavy burden becomes bearable through the fact that I know that my election (for no reason) does not mean that another is rejected (for no reason), but that I, who fail, who am impotent, am *used* where I no longer see any effect. The fruit that the vine brings forth from the chosen one is not used for him but for the refreshment of the other one, dying of thirst, for the deliverance of the world.

It may indeed seem very paradoxical that this idea should emerge precisely at the moment when the Church as a whole seems engaged in gathering her forces on the inside and keeping them together. Is it not madness to lay upon a pastor the responsibility for the Protestants, Jews and pagans who live in his territory, at the very moment when he is no longer able even to cope with the majority of non-practicing Catholics (who increase in numbers every day)? Is not such an ideal construction in itself an ideology, indeed the expression of a hidden defeatism on the level of reality, and is not this characteristic once again of the delicate, perhaps already utopian situation of the Church in our world? Napoleon never dreamed greater dreams than in the memoirs he wrote on St. Helena. And did not Buddhism and Islam too begin to develop a spiritualist and universalist theology at the time when their penetrating force in the earthly realm was already half broken? Are we not therefore engaging in an armchair universalism? Not in the least. The deepening of Christian consciousness in the modern era can be demonstrably traced to the earliest Christian sources: this deepening penetrates through to authentic matters that become evident in the Gospel only now, but now with full clarity. With equal clarity one could demonstrate why what is now being disclosed remained hidden for so long (and these reasons lie outside the Gospel). Thus it is not a case of sublimation but a return to what is genuine.

Now that the outer shells are falling away, they can be called by their worldly names. Once again, the Church is at the beginning. She was never given the promise of a quantitative superiority. The limits imposed at the time of the Reformation could very well be understood as the forced return from an illusion to a truth—or at least as an image of this. And the external reduction (paralleled, as has been shown, by an inner and spiritual reduction) was the necessary prerequisite for understanding the new function of the Church as the yeast of the world: a function that quite naturally is understood much better in the diaspora than in Catholic countries. This is beginning to be understood by the Church as a whole, now that she is (like the primitive Church) moving toward a situation of diaspora once again. This is the moment when for the first time responsibility for the world and apostolate takes hold of every member of the Church as something self-evident; what the parish priest, or indeed any official representative of the hierarchy, is no longer able to do must now be done by the layman—and this "must" falls with the weight of a fundamental duty.

A second train of thought enters here. The Lord has said to his Church, "You are the light of the world." Light does not shine for itself but for the beginners who need it in order to flourish, to see, to grow, to warm themselves. The light of the abstract, timeless truth is indeed always present; it is never exhausted. But one cannot say of it that it radiates itself. It was through his miracles that Christ, although he was God and the personal Light of the world, shone forth: "a power went forth from him"; indeed, his freely given light went forth to meet an hour of darkness with the power of that life which was his to live and to pour out upon men—that life seemed exhausted and drained out in Christ himself. This was no physical or physiological process, for Christ also possessed the power "to take up his life again", although he preferred to wait until the Father restored it to him. But it is a wholly real process called by the Church Fathers the "wondrous exchange": He is dead so that we may live, his light is extinguished so that the darkness in us may become bright. In all this he is bearing our death, our darkness, so that the exchange may be perfect.

But if the Church is not only the passive result of Christ's act of redemption (that is, not only light, where he is darkness), but the consort who helps him, must not something of Christ's mystery be repeated in her too? Many truths, once possessed only by the Church, have somehow been scattered abroad, becoming humanity's common property—human rights, for example. (In most cases, this process has gone unrecognized.) Down through the ages, the Church has been radiating, transmitting these truths, and they have penetrated the organism of mankind, becoming light and strength.

And again, one can ask whether that fragment-littered field—littered with the ruins of churches lying between *Catholica* and the world—does not form a kind of transition, a bridge; considered thus it takes on a different and more positive significance: that of bearing the light of truth to be shed into the world; no longer central, and indeed clouded, darkened, falsified; nevertheless, still light that would not exist if the central light were not there; a light on its knees, light that already is almost prostrate on the ground; beneficent light that has the power to penetrate still darker, yet more lost, corners. (For every twilight encounters a still darker night.) And so much is this the case, that the inner light seems weak and wavering because of the light that is dawning outside. Now at last what Paul said to his Corinthians holds good for the whole Church in her relationship to the world: "We are fools for Christ, but you are the reasonable ones in Christ; we are weak, you are strong; you are in honor, we are without honor." And so that this may be true, he, as Church, takes the responsibility of suffering upon himself: "We are cursed, and we bless; we are persecuted and we permit it; we are calumniated and we console. We have become the scum of the earth, refuse in everyone's eyes up to the present day" (1 Cor 4:10–13).

If this were the key to the present situation of the Church then she would stand closer to the Lord in the active event of redemption than ever before. It would also be true then that her apparent organic weakness, her decline, her division belong in reality to the mystery of a supernatural weakening corresponding, in its own time, to an exalted supernatural fruitfulness. And even if it seems one could almost calculate how much of her actual substance the Church has delivered over (for example, to the heresies which have borne off whole portions of truth from her); even if it is true, as Yves Congar demonstrates, that this real loss, though not indicating that the Church has been robbed of any essential Catholic truth, does still mean that she has been robbed of a vital integrity (because the Church must naturally answer one-sided positions with counter-positions); nevertheless, the saints in their turn show that the fullness of the Church's truth is lacking in nothing, and that indeed the Holy Spirit is able to restore the Church (which had almost bled to death) to her vigorous power of life in a superabundant manner.

The mystery, then, of the supernatural loss which constitutes the redemption, can in no way be reckoned here on earth. No one can say how such losses on the part of Christ, donor of divine blood to the world from its very beginning, were balanced; and these losses are no figure of speech, since they were collected in the vessels of bodily men, and lived as something they gained, and still more because these losses were experienced as such by one bodily Man; rather, they are the realism of the *instrumentum conjunctum*, the flesh and spirit of Jesus made use of for the lowliest work of cleansing the world. "A power went forth from him and healed them all" (Lk 6:19); "he healed many, so that all who were tormented by sufferings pressed forward to him, in order to touch him" (Mk 3:10);

"and at once, Jesus felt in himself that a power had gone forth from him, and he turned round in the crowd and said, 'Who has touched my garments?' " (Mk 5:30).

Once again, the mediation of grace is no abstraction, but a living event felt in the exhaustion of the one who gives beyond all measure; the *quaerens me sedisti lassus* corresponds to a subjective experience permeating the whole of the Redeemer's existence, becoming, not only at the end, not only in the decisive loss of substance in the winepress of the Cross, the experience of the night. Nevertheless, the Son looks to the Father up to that point, and receives in love all the love of the Father that he gives further to others, and he gives the Father everything (even the little love that he receives from the world), and because love lives from giving, this act of giving strengthens him and nourishes him.

One must look to this incalculable oscillation between boundless strength and extremest weariness, in order to sense what Paul states with unsurpassable clarity: "When I am weak, then I am strong." The instruction came to him from the Lord himself: "My grace is enough for you, for power attains its perfection in weakness." Power becomes strongest where it no longer encounters any contrary power in the one who mediates it, only the pure will to accept and surrender. And this power does not stand in any antithesis to the

weakness in which one is not able to offer resis-
tance, for it comes from the weakness of the Cross
and is the power of weakness itself. When Paul
"takes pleasure in weakness, ill-treatment, distress,
persecution and anxieties for the sake of Christ . . .
so that the power of Christ may make its home in
me" (2 Cor 12:9–10), all the things he lists are connected with power in Christ himself; all of them,
up to and including the anxiety in which all the
weaknesses gather and are dammed up, are the
forms of his power, always ready to emerge once
again into the light where the power of Christ is
communicated (for example, in Holy Communion). But Holy Communion, as an individual "sacrament", is only the particular expression of what
continually occurs, without any possibility of inter-
ruption, in the primal sacrament of the nuptial
union between Christ and the Church: the nup-
tiality of the Incarnate God with humanity, of
which the overpowering of the woman in relation
to the man is an image. Weakness means fruitfulness; and the weakness of the Bride Church in the
face of the peoples is a mystery of her fruit-bearing
among them, a mystery that remains invisible to
eyes outside her.

It is necessary that she should not feel the power
that goes forth from her in any way other than as a
loss of power, and also that she should not know
who among the crowd of the people has touched
her: one person among millions, or the throng of

the millions themselves, or perhaps the one who is weakest and most ill among these millions, hoping to remain undiscovered in the crowd like the woman with the flow of blood. And who will this weakest of all be but her Bridegroom, unrecognizable under the mask of the least of men? Without knowing to whom she gives herself, the Church lets her powers flow: "then the righteous will answer him and say, 'Lord, when did we see you hungry, and give you food? Or when did we see you thirsty, and give you drink? Or naked, and clothe you? When did we see you sick or in prison, and come to you?'" (Mt 25:37–39).

Both these trains of thought have attempted to plot the course of the shift in Christian awareness since the middle ages. Both circle around the idea of fellowship in destiny, the dominating idea in our age. The blossom that has opened in the Church will not close again. If we look back to the middle ages, we see it still closed. Some things were possible then that are no longer possible today. It was possible to be a wonderfully awake Christian like Dante and yet pass through the hell of his fellow Christians with a hardened heart and unmoved, contemplating the tortures of this most impressive of all concentration camps, studying them, committing them to memory, letting life-stories and tragedies be related to him and each time shaking the dust from his feet at the end, passing on, leaving behind what could not be changed and leaving it to itself. What a Christian of that era could justify, cannot be accepted today; otherwise, he would reveal himself to be an utter un-Christian. For in the meantime something new has been displayed among us. The medieval castle where people danced and gorged themselves in the festival hall above the deep dungeons and torture chambers has collapsed and will not be reconstructed. And no Christian today will be able to dance any longer, while one of his brothers is suffering torture.

But has theology kept pace with this change, or is not Christian life several leaps ahead of it? Many are ready today to give their life for the Church and the world (and not at all for their own perfection). They would stand in need of a theology that describes Christian existence from the perspective of service, of the commission received, of sharing both in the shining and radiating and in the being consumed. If such a theology were once clearly thought out and popularized so that it too could take its place in Christian instruction, new power could radiate forth from the Christian communities into the world. Further, how could it be forgotten that the revelation of the riches of Christ has infinitely more fullness than all the concepts and structures of every theology and of every Christian consciousness at any period at all? Let us therefore not cling tightly to structures of thought, but let us plunge into the primal demands of the Gospel, which are also the primal graces, visible and capable of being grasped in the example of Christ, who gave himself for all in order to save all.

III

ENDURANCE

The new position of the Church vis-à-vis the world augers an ever deeper and more serious incarnation. But just as the Son of God, the more he became a man (until he appeared only as a naked man on the Cross), did not lose his Godhead and indeed revealed it with ever greater clarity (until its incomprehensibility broke out, unconcealed, in the night of the Cross), so the Church's position will become similarly paradoxical through her deeper entering into the world. And those representatives of the Church's authority who summon and welcome the Church's descent and who encourage the laity to join in the work with a professional competence all their own must be clearly aware of the theological consequences of this summons, so that it may not become the invocation of the sorcerer's apprentice.

The Church remains at every period what she was: the bulwark and the steward of all truth, for all the treasures of wisdom and knowledge are hidden in Christ, and no one has access to these treasures of Christ except through the Church. But when she enters into the world and becomes for the world one religion among others, one community among others, one doctrine and truth among others—just as Christ became one man among others, outwardly indistinguishable from them— her truth comes into a communism with all the forms of worldly truth: with the experiential truth of all branches of knowledge, and with the wisdom-systems of the world which attempt conclusive statements about the being of the world and of its truth.

The collision is something given with the very mission of the Church; it happened already in Alexandria in the third century, where Christianity had to try its strength against Plato and Philo; in the thirteenth century, when Aristotle came into theology's sights as the leading star of the rising modern empiricism; in the fifteenth and sixteenth centuries, when the entire classical age rose up anew, the sciences developed, the historical religions of the various peoples came into view. Since then, this progress has continued into our own day, with the world's knowledge spread out like a delta that no one can take in at a single glance. It has become impossible today for anyone to do what was still just possible for an individual in the middle ages: namely, to have an overview, and to summarize everything in the synthesizing peak of theology: one could, at any time, from the highest watchtower atop the world-cone, look out, *oneself unmoving*, at all the movement (like Dante from Paradise, or like Camões' Vasco da Gama or the

Mexican nun from her heavenly sphere). But now that the world has become spherical, there is no longer any place from which one's gaze can take in everything; one must *set oneself in motion*: the only way to explore the land of truth is by changing one's standpoint.

This exclusively modern experience—that the different realms of truth demand a change of one's intellectual standpoint (an experience given clear expression by Hegel's dialectics, Bergson's and Dilthey's intellectual philosophy of life and of understanding, and Husserl's phenomenology)— reinforces in an exceptional manner the necessity of trust in intellectual matters. Specialization in the different areas is necessarily the socialization of those who work in these areas: the more detailed a person's research becomes and the more of his life he dedicates to his object of study, the more difficult it becomes to check his work and the more necessary it is to assume his honesty. Even if his results are accepted by science in general, it is not possible for another (to say nothing of *all* others) to take once more the path he has taken. It is indeed necessary for the results to be demonstrated, and these proofs are like representative cross-sections through his investigation, exposing its correctness for everyone to see.

But perhaps all that these proofs give is a summary insight, and he himself, with the unrepeatable experience of the time spent in service of the matter, remains the only genuine specialist in his object of study. Other tracks through the woods of scholarship can be more public, and the paths taken (as in the case of mathematics) can be followed in turn by anyone who takes the necessary time and effort. But then another form of esotericism is produced on the part of those who do in fact go to the trouble of paying the price of this time and effort—and there will be only a few of these, especially where the object of study is recondite. Thus we come to a fine and humane (in the best sense) balance between objectivity and honesty in the great field of human investigation: objectivity is the virtue that can be checked, that reveals itself in the object studied, whereas honesty is the virtue presupposed, which depends on the person and reveals itself in the objectivity.

A lack of objectivity, deceit and falsehood for the sake of propaganda are things that the coming generations will reject fundamentally, like a sickness; and the more mankind becomes one, and is dependent on the honesty of all, the more inexorably will it be necessary to reject these. Furthermore, this socialization yields a perspective of the field of truth that only increases as science progresses: the world as a whole has a different countenance for the natural scientist than for the one who is engaged in the study of the humanities; it looks different from the perspective of the doctor, of the factory worker, of the theologian. The theologian, who once could presume to take an "overview", stands today, in one specific and not unimportant sense, as one specialist alongside *others*.

This has significant consequences both for the theoretical relationship between the truth of revelation and worldly truth, and for the practical, peaceable coexistence of their representatives.

The theoretical problem is first of all to be found in the Christian himself. In the study of a secular science or in carrying out a secular profession or in his relations with persons whose horizon is totally determined by worldly truth he can become uncertain as to where in fact the axis, the center of his own truth, is to be found. The more he penetrates his area, the more he finds his own view of the world elliptic, and this precisely when he remains alive as a Christian, when he prays, contemplates and receives the sacraments with alert faith. It is important to know that this feeling of a "double truth", which usually comes on precisely the best and most enthusiastic students, is not the sign of something improper. The two perspectives that split apart here can no more be made to coincide with one another than can divine and human truth, Church and world, or the divine and the human natures in Christ and the manner of knowledge proper to each of these natures in him. The Christian is charged absolutely to bear this tension and extension, but also increasingly to bring it under control and to clear a path for himself through it. On the level of experience, this may not initially succeed (and perhaps not for a long time), and he retains the feeling that he literally crosses into "another world" as he goes from the spiritual arena (for example, early Mass) to the secular arena (for example, the lecture hall). Nevertheless, even now the synthesis must be established in the clarity of the path, in the act of *going* from the one to the other—for it is a path taken in the Christian commission, and thus a path of Christ, even and precisely in its changes of standpoint—until gradually the decisiveness of the act of going becomes a thoroughly matured Christian experience and wisdom, and generates of itself a superior form of the truth, attained through suffering and put to the test.

The secular researcher and worker too knows something of such a maturation process, and the experience the Christian shares with those who follow the same procession will be a genuinely common experience, even if his Christian standpoint forbids and prevents the horizon of secular truth from closing in on itself and resting in itself. The feeling a Christian student often has, which he experiences only from the outside, in an "as if", what his unbelieving colleagues experience from the inside (and seemingly much more truly), is ultimately false; the objective truth of these secular things is not a truth closed in on itself, but a truth that is opened toward Christ, and it is a preliminary truth. Where there is not a subjective experience both of this objective opening and of transcendence, there exists in reality a deficiency, not an advantage, even if the strength of the experience appears to be intensified by the very lack of transcendence.

It may be that one has, as a Christian, the feeling that in order "to experience from the inside" certain poets (especially modern poets like Baudelaire or Rilke), one ought to close the windows that open upon the supernatural. This may indeed by partly the case, because the poet's world itself came into being with the windows closed, and that certain dullness of subjectivity is necessary in order to recreate it precisely in one's own experience. Yet the genuine Christian will sense the brackets set around this "world-interior" with all its inner "infinity". He has a need to breathe in the greater space of God and of Christ, and so his will not to let himself be locked into this inner room is no infidelity to the "truth" of the poet or of poetry as a whole, or of the world as a whole. As he matures in his specialty he will become convinced of this: for after he has gone through the stage of the dull subjectivity that enjoys its own self and is mostly melancholic, he comes to see panoramas he has till now overlooked: beside his hitherto "favorite poets" he comes to see the breadth of world literature, with its own coolness and objectivity; he becomes aware of linguistics, and in this the distance from the individual form of expression, as well as the relativization of styles and of the ideals of beauty.

In a similar way, the doctor achieves a distance from the science of his teacher, of his school, of his age, from the image of man that was unconsciously presupposed there; as he wanders through the broad spaces of his faculty, he will discover the preliminary character of all knowledge and for this reason, if he is not a believer, he can easily become a sceptic. For the non-believer, whether he admits it or not, will fundamentally orient himself in terms of an ideal of timeless, systematic truth, and every relativity that is conditioned by history seems to him to be a loss of the certainty and reliability of the truth. For the Christian, who comes out of historical revelation, this ought not really to be the case.

The concept of truth that man had in the Old Testament was based on God's reliability, on his faithfulness, his covenant, his promise. Every man remained opened to receive this God, and God could inscribe on this openness what he wished, something new and unexpected, and precisely the character of newness was evidence in each case for the genuineness of the revelation. God's truth was always his deed within time, and reflection on the greatness of this deed was, for the holy people, what reflection on the truth of God in creation—systematic philosophy—was for the Gentiles.

With Christ, God posits his greatest and most unexpected deed, and it is out of the question that the truth of revelation would have been transferred through Christ from the form of the reality of deed and history into the form of ahistorical systematics. On the contrary, as the Jew was one led by God's truth, so the Christian remains, to an even greater extent, one handed over and given up to God's creative working in Christ through the Holy Spirit. He knows the perspective of the fullness of Christ, which appears to him anew every morning—not only subjectively, but also objectively—and gives itself to him anew. The Spirit blows where he wills, Christ gives what he wills, the Father demands and takes as he wills, but the Christian stands defenseless in the midst of this billowing truth and is yielded up to every wave that breaks on him. He cannot conceal himself behind any truth that might cover him, to protect himself from a truth of God. He cannot use any known truth (to say nothing of a whole system) as a weapon against the unknown, infallible truth of God that now assaults him. The living Christian ought therefore to be accustomed to encounter the perspectives of ecclesiastical truth and secular truth without becoming frightened, since he comes from the most living truth of all. The "infallibility" of the divine truth (which infallibly intends him and makes demands of him) does not stand in opposition to the historical character of its vitality, and therefore the same is true of the ecclesiastical infallibility which represents it.

And thus, out of the continual act of walking between faith and knowledge, an equilibrium between Christian and worldly truth, or more precisely, between ecclesiastical "infallibility" and human, scientific "tolerance", comes into being for him. This equilibrium comes about when he endures and tolerates (*tolerare*) the limited character of worldly truth in himself and in others—and this can be a genuine burden for the one who knows about the infallibility of Christian truth (a burden not at all felt by the others, who are "tolerant" a priori). At the same time, he must not confuse the "infallibility" of Christian truth with an immovability of its human position or attribute to it functions that it can never fulfill and that Christ least of all claimed for himself: namely, from an immovable position, to anticipate, judge and even render superfluous all the experiences of the world— experiences gained only when one is oneself in motion.

Christ himself was "in motion": he was not at home anywhere on earth, he was a wandering rabbi without a home, without the den of the foxes or the nest of the bird, without a cushion to rest his head, without ever having the prospect of returning to his own home. Nor was his food a solid, supratemporal truth-system, but the will of the Father at each instant. He walked in the light of this will, just as those who imitate him are to walk after him, that they may not walk in the darkness: they are to "walk in faith" (2 Cor 5:7), "walk in the Spirit" (Rom 8:4), "walk in the day" (Jn 11:9), "walk in love" (Eph 5:2), "walk in Jesus" (Col 2:6). Thus "they walk in a way worthy of God" (Col 1:10). There exists no other form of "abiding" here than that of walking: "Anyone who says that he abides in him, must himself walk in the way that he walked" (1 Jn 2:6).

"Walking" is a fundamental category of biblical and Christian existence: apart from walking, there is no certainty, no grasping of the truth, no standing fast. Christ himself fulfills the Old Testament attitude of walking before God, and he does this with all the mobility and flexibility of life that was expressed in this attitude. And only the one who walks remains related to Christ. The shepherd walks ahead, those who are "outside" hear his voice and walk after him (Jn 10:4): more hearing than seeing, more groping, feeling, scenting, than immovably assured: the one who walks has the strongest feeling of living. And so the Church too walks; yes, even the "rock" shared in the walking in the desert of old (1 Cor 10:4), so how could she not walk after Christ the rock, as the new rock? The rock is at the same time a wobbling boat; the vessel that cannot be conquered is at the same time a ship that is wrecked, the planks of which are yet sufficient to bring one safely to land (Acts 27:44);

the rigid framework is at the same time a flexible, supple and growing body that "grows upwards", with ligaments and joints that stretch, and that builds itself up until it attains the full age of Christ (Eph 4:13f.). The individual learns, as he shares in this divine walking in the world, to sense God's walking past (*passah*) in the changes of the world's situation. He learns that what counts is not the rigid synthesis of two rigid truths, as perhaps he dreamed initially, but that unity is a movement problem.

And this very personal problem, which the individual Christian struggles through and solves in himself, opens him up to a problem between men, particularly between the theologian, as the "specialist" in the infallible truth of God, and the specialist in any one field of worldly truth. The question has many layers; let us separate these.

1. In the earlier example it was the "layman" working within a secular branch of knowledge and coming up against its limits; he grasps its relativity and so discovers the place where the truth of revelation could have an illuminating and guiding function in the domain of the secular. But one can just as well begin with the "theologian", who comes up against the relativity of human words and concepts at every turn—for example, in contemporary biblical scholarship, in the history of dogma, in the history of theological ethics. Perhaps he observes this fact with pain, perhaps with sur-

prise; and yet he must reconcile and unite this fact with the continuous validity of revelation, on the one hand, and its essential expression in dogma on the other. This experience becomes even stronger when he emerges into living pastoral work equipped with the abstract knowledge of the seminary, when the spiritual truth is to be applied to a secular humanity. Thus he will not at all be one to lay exclusive claim to infallibility for himself, while leaving the wide perspectives of worldly truth to the non-theologian. Both of them undergo essentially the same elliptical "double experience", even if they come from opposite poles. Both are essentially en route, disturbed out of their calm, occupied with a synthesis that can never be fully achieved.

2. The disturbance experienced by the theologian in his own domain is intensified when the question is raised of the relationship between theology and the other sciences. On his own he cannot so delimit the relationship as to give everything the appearance of a priori regularity, forestalling any future "surprises". He had always conceded the secular sciences a certain autonomy, but he was nonetheless surprised to see that the Galileo affair compelled a painful retreat in theology's claims to infallibility in the secular domain, surprised too to see that modern archaeology, palaeontology, Oriental studies, et cetera, still make theology hold its breath and keep it in sus-

pense. The current bewilderment of German Protestant theology confronted with Bultmann's problem of "demythologization" is only one particularly acute symptom of the confrontation that never comes to a stop but continues into the most fundamental questions. If it were otherwise, if the field of the contents and expression of the infallible truth had been marked off rigidly once and for all against all that is mutable, then people would long since have lost interest in this question and would have ceased to grant the Christian truth any competence in secular concerns.

3. In accordance with what has been said above, the movement between the two areas since the middle ages has advanced particularly in one direction: the way in which the simple predominance of theology was supplemented through the equally-ranked order of secular studies, or (and this amounts to the same thing) the way in which the barriers between the *civitas Dei* and the *civitas terrena* have fallen in favor of a newly-perceived solidarity, in the earthly realm and in the spiritual realm. The only consequence of this can be that, alongside the "professional experience" of the Christian who is a theologian, the "professional experience" of the Christian layman—who is not a theologian, but a doctor, jurist, businessman or worker—gains in position and significance in its own autonomy. The element of trust, so needed today when the individual can no longer com-

mand an overview of the totality of human experience, receives a new place within Christianity too. To the extent that the Christian in the world recognizes and accepts his position between divine and human truths as a position of utterly original responsibility that cannot be equated with any other responsibility, his Christian experience of life will be a piece of Christianity indispensable to the total experience of the Church, something that, as a wisdom that is at any rate "lived" and based on experience, has just as much claim to validity as the more theoretical wisdom of the theologians. This is why cooperation between theologians and laymen, for example in the form of a "lay council" for bishops and pastors, is something demanded not only by the practical-minded Catholic Action, but also by the Church's theology which is to be read from the hour now sounding in the world.

4. Behind the encounter between the theologian and the layman there stands the Church, embracing both as her members, the Church which guards and expounds the infallible truth of God in the world. But her task is more than keeping watch over conceptual formulas; just as much, and even more so, she must watch over Christian life, and her verdict is infallible, not only in matters of the faith, but also in matters of ethics. What is ultimately and before all else infallible is God in the grace that, in Christ, became a man, and this grace is preserved by the Church both in its essential and

in its existential truth: what she proclaims infallibly in her teaching, she lives infallibly and visibly in her holiness, in her saints (despite all human weakness), for otherwise she could not infallibly canonize the course of their lives. An essential part of this existential truth is an authentic Christian experience of worldly truth: the endurance of the alien character of this truth, of its inadaptibility to the sacred inner room of the divine truth out of which Christ and the Church live and in which they are at home. It belongs to the Christian life in the world that one must endure this alien character; indeed, it belongs in an original sense to the sacrifice that God makes in the Incarnation, and thus the Church's endurance or tolerance is ultimately a part of her Cross: the enduring and bearing of this alien burden, just as the Lord himself bore it when he took upon himself "life among this perverse generation" (Mt 17:17) and did not shrink from contact with its foreign, darkened and distorted truth, condescending again and again in his words and in his experiences to make the journey from his own innate truth to its truth.

When it is a matter of the inviolable truth of God, one cannot depart even a little from the intolerance incumbent upon the Church and achieved in her through obedience; one can praise the Church as the one shelter of the truth in the midst of a surging sea of error and unbounded relativity (as Maritain has rightly done); one can attribute to this ecclesiastical truth a certain iron hardness proper to the charism of caring for the truth, as the most salutary medicine for an over-indulged human race, and one will be correct to do so. Nonetheless, if the Church is properly to be all this and do all this, one can look calmly only if the lighthouse from whose tower the beams sweep over the turbulent waters is at its base washed by these same waves; if the open intransigence, to which the Church is called, is itself paid for with a hidden endurance, a genuine involvement with all the forms of human experience of the world, not excluding the most alien forms, so that not only the sinners but also the saints, also the Church's members whom she protects and shields—and they with a yet deeper right—are able to join Christ their Head in saying the *nil humanum mihi alienum puto*. Thus, drenched with the bitterest gall of the world's truth, earning the unity of all this truth in God through her thirst for unity, while in the world's night everything threatens only to break up into ever more alien and hostile parts, thus drawn into the experience of the Cross which is the self-alienation of truth (until truth and truth no longer know one another, and find no longer any path to one another), she matures to become the power that unites from within what has become separated.

Here would be the place to speak of the great return home of the heresies, and further of the return home of the religions and the philosophies. The Church must cut herself off from much in intransigence, and she must condemn much and declare anathema much with which, in the dark, she remains in communion, just as Christ himself can make a judgment about the sinner only because he has, from within, experienced, known and borne away the sinner's darkness. In the New Covenant, there is no longer any other way, not even for the ministerial Church, to judge than by suffering inwardly with the brother who is judged. In this hidden interior begins the return home of all truth to the *Una Catholica*: the truth of Goethe, the truth of Nietzsche, the truth of Luther, and of all who took up a fragment of the infinite mirror. For all who have erred did at one time intend to speak the truth. And the reconstruction of the smashed mirror is not the outcome of a game of patience (like Hegel's *Encyclopaedia*), but the outcome of the miracle of Easter, in which the patient endurance of the Church too plays its part. Rightly, the motto of worldly tolerance, "To understand everything is to forgive everything", has been rejected as superficial. But perhaps the reversal of this motto is valid, at a much deeper point: where everything is first forgiven (on the Cross), even what is most incomprehensible becomes understandable; the hard outer shells of error break open and release the captive kernel of truth. The tolerance of this world is weak; the judgment of the Church is hard. But it is hard only because the judgment of the Cross is hard; and all who are to share in judging at the judgment of the Son of Man must be unsparingly judged in this judgment of the Cross, together with him and the world.

And now, the practical side for the individual. We have first the question of Christian caution and carefreeness, and then the question about Christian impatience and patience. Caution more in bearing the divine truth than in enduring the worldly truth: if everything is pure to the one who is pure, then he need not impose on himself any anxious concern about contamination, *as long as* he is pure. Priests and persons in religious life often worry unnecessarily about the Christians in the world in this area. Where there is a Christian, there is the Church; he bears the light with him, and therefore (as long as he bears it truly) he never comes into an area outside the Church. The Fathers were accustomed to marvel as they compared the divine truth with light, which illuminates the lowliest places without soiling itself. The same is true of the Christian in the world. "Whatever is lit up by the light, is light" (Eph 5:12). And where a child of God and member of his household enters, that place becomes a home to him, since it has its origin from the Father and belongs to the realm of the Son. Nevertheless, it belongs to Christian existence in a world still only en route to full redemption, that the rift between light and darkness, inside and outside, goes right through the path and through the interior consciousness of the Christian, and that Paul insists on caution (Eph 5:15), Peter on watchful sobriety (1 Pet 5:8) and the Lord even on fear of the evil one and of his power (Mt 10:28). This is why there is no secular analogy for the paradox that the Christian goes out into the alien darkness with caution and not without strong weapons, and yet takes this same path with the carefreeness of a child skipping along.

The tension between impatience and patience is even less explicable. Impatience with this world that does not understand God's truth; impatience that it is so deaf and so sluggish, so venal and lecherous; that it does not even feel the goad with which God pursues it; that all it can say, when God's voice resounds clearly and mightily from heaven, is: "It has thundered" (Jn 12:29); and that, where the whip of the Son of God strikes it, it scatters for a moment and then presumably installs itself next day in the same place in the temple. Without this impatience on the part of God and of Christ and of the Christian, Christian patience would not be what it ought to be: a "nevertheless", a bearing of what is unbearable, an abiding on this alien soil which refuses to take on any of the qualities of a homeland. A holding out in a night that shows no sign of ending. An endless wandering through the wilderness.

Augustine used all these images time and again: he knew well how the citizen of Jerusalem felt in the meadows of Babylon. Even if the relationship between Church and world has shifted since his time, the paradox remains the same, and can indeed become only more pointed. The same kingdom that "sprouts and grows by day and by night, without one's noticing it" (Mk 4:28) must be snatched by the violent for themselves. This is the unity of the suffering "let it be" and incisive decisiveness, the unity of Christian tolerance and Christian intransigence.

Thus severity and mildness belong together in the Church's enactments: a prudently yielding diplomacy and a rigidity that is apparently without experience of the world. Both hierarchy and laity must unite the two sides in themselves, even if in practice tolerance is more the affair of the laity, and holding fast to the forms and formulas of revelation and tradition is more the affair of the hierarchy and its representatives. The laity, especially today, are the element projecting into the world, and they will more frequently convince the hierarchy to apply a new tolerance. The hierarchy will not so much seek to restrain the conquering troops as to equip them with sufficient knowledge of Christian truth and experience of life. The official Church has of course the right and the duty to lay down certain rules to determine Christian tolerance and its limits. She has always done so, and she has done this anew in her code of canon law and books of moral theology. But these rules, which must be followed, never take the place of the spirit in which they are carried out. And what is at issue here is this spirit: this alert, clear unity of generosity and decisiveness, which can truly be achieved only out of living prayer and is the opposite of a vague, unclarified attitude that confuses things spiritually and intellectually incompatible.

How both can be united is ultimately God's mystery: in his act of election, he separates a holy space from a profane space, in order then to redeem the profane through the holy; God is righteous and punishes, and yet he is loving and remits the punishment; he protects what is holy with flaming jealousy, and yet pours it into the unholy world as if nonchalantly. For when did God not cast pearls before the swine? When did he not "bend the rules a bit", like the unrighteous steward whom he praises? Thus the solution lies in the power and purity of the heart, which clarifies in itself what is impure and justly looks on it as pure. The God-Man has the heart, and Christians listen eagerly to its beating.

IV

CONTACT

If all this is true, then *sentire cum Ecclesia*, "thinking with the Church", has likewise changed since the middle ages. Two things have come into being at the same time, and these ought to be mentioned and seen together: first, when the Church emerges from a splendid isolation and enters the tumult of the age, she receives a new contact with the cares and hopes of mankind as a whole; and second, the more the individual himself, especially the layman, takes on ecclesial responsibility, the more deeply he feels with the Church, indeed, on an ever deeper level, he feels himself to be the Church. In both cases we see how little that is fundamentally new is involved in these changes, and how much it is only the oldest material of the tradition taken up, purified and used anew.

Let us begin with the second point: the more the layman, or member of the Church in general, takes on Christian responsibility, which means ecclesial responsibility, the more strongly does he feel himself to be Church. For the Church is no *universale ante rem*: she is entirely embodied in her members, as humanity is embodied in each man, even if not all the members give expression to the

Church's nature in the same way (just as man and woman, or youth and old age, are different and mutually exclusive presentations of the one common nature). Because the Church (also in her social being) is always present where there is a genuine Christian, and the more purely his Christian existence shines forth and becomes incarnated, the more purely the idea of the Church shines forth, it follows that the Church is present in her purest idea in the bodily Mother and spiritual Bride of the Lord: in Mary. Thus, if one speaks of "ecclesial attitude", one must mean the attitude that filled Mary, since she is the embodiment of the Church as lived reality. It is vitally important to go back to this center-point; thus we destroy any impression that "ecclesial attitude" is primarily a catchword for the listening Church in her relationship to the teaching Church. Obedience is not an attribute of the "people of the Church" alone, but is the attribute of Ecclesia as a whole, precedent to her differentiation into a teaching and a listening part, of the Ecclesia-Mary, as the handmaid of the Lord, to whom it is done according to the word of the Lord, who ponders in her heart all the words of the Lord in order to nourish herself on them, who sits at the feet of Jesus and has chosen the best part, who breaks her urn of ointment so that it may serve the Bridegroom as oil to anoint him, and who stands silently under the Cross in order to be led into the mysteries of all fruitfulness.

Ecclesial obedience is in its origin and in truth the obedience of the Church to her Lord; this is why feeling with the Church means feeling in oneself this obedience of the Church. Not by chance did Ignatius of Loyola, in his first "Rule for Thinking with the Church", link obedience vis-à-vis the Church's authority both to the nuptial character of the Church and to her maternal character: "By leaving aside every private judgment we must keep our spirit ready and willing to obey in everything the true Bride of Christ our Lord, who is our holy Mother, the hierarchical Church." The hierarchical Church (which is not exactly the same thing as the hierarchy in the Church) can receive the commission to guide her members only out of her own submission to the Lord and Spirit who guides her, and the only way for her to carry out this charge is to mediate this spirit of service to her members.

It is something natural for the Catholic that this innermost hierarchical attitude also presents itself visibly and externally as obedience to the hierarchy: this is the test of the presence of the inner attitude, something that fully corresponds to the order of Incarnation, and it is indeed the only way that the absoluteness, totality and boundlessness of Christ's obedience in relation to the Father (through which he redeemed the world) can be seriously imitated in his mystical Body and its members. And one should note that the concept

(so difficult for a Protestant to accept) of an immediate "imitation of Christ" in obedience, and thus
in the order of co-redemption, is dialectically
broken and brought into the necessary distance of
reverence precisely through the idea of the Marian
handmaid-character of the Church as a whole.
There is no need to employ the demanding term
"imitation of Christ"; it is enough to have the attitude of the Mother of the Lord and to be in contact with her: ready and available for everything,
even when the signal is given to set out on the
way of the Cross.

Mary's obedience is not an obedience that is
emphasized, emerging as a theme in its own right
alongside the obedience of the Son; rather, it is an
utterly secondary obedience which seconds him
and is in this sense imitable. This is also why her
ruling (as Queen of Heaven and the Lady Ecclesia)
cannot become a theme in its own right alongside
the Son's ruling—as another, a second, subordi-
nated or juxtaposed authority which one would
also have to obey; rather, everything is included in
her pointing to the Son. One could object that the
authority of the men who form the hierarchy in
the Church derives directly from Christ and does
not pass via Mary even in an indirect and mediate
manner, and that, as a woman, she has nothing to
do with the Church's hierarchy. But even the
hierarchy and its explicitly masculine functions
remain embraced within the servant reality of the

whole Church, of the woman giving birth in Revelation 12 (who gives birth also to the men with their hierarchical offices), and of the spouse of the Lamb, whose idea and real symbol is Mary; and it is she who must regulate and dictate the character and tenor of the hierarchical function of regulating and dictating.

Thus "Marian" piety can only be ecclesial piety, particularly in the sense that any and all externality in the formula *sentire cum Ecclesia* be increasingly drawn into the interiority of a genuine *sentire Ecclesiae* in each individual Christian. To express this point in Hegel's categories: the essence of the Church (as Mary) emerges from the externality of a merely venerating "devotion" to Mary as a privileged individual, so as to become internalized, both in the Church as a whole and in the individual within her—and both processes can only occur in complete simultaneity. Naturally, since Mary is an individual person, she also remains an individual and external "model", a model that points beyond itself in its appearing, and thus disappears. But because she is essence, her form is imparted to the Church and to the individual, and therefore she takes on a special visibility, becoming for the Church of today the object of special reflection. To repeat: this imparting of the form of the image of the serving Bride, when it is authentic, can never lead the individual to the delusion that he is now the Church (for that would mean the absurd confusion of himself with the Bride without spot or stain, with the Immaculate Conception!) and has perhaps then passed beyond hierarchical obedience into a zone or a Joachimite epoch of ecclesial maturity and self-awareness. One glance at Mary, who was submissive to the Lord and subsequently to the Apostle John, suffices to dismiss such humbug. Thus the Catholic will always remain in a childlike attitude with respect to the visible governors of the Church's ordered structure and the dispensers of Word and sacrament.

Nevertheless, when the Marian element awakens in the Church, the listening Church and the teaching Church find one another in the common matrix of ecclesial feeling, and there inevitably occurs a drawing closer together. We see this in the way the one who hears now takes up his own responsibility for the Word of God (Biblical Movement) and bears this Word out into a world which is far from God, into far distant places where the priestly word no longer reaches; and equally in the way the hierarchical word (for example, of the reigning Pope) emerges from its sublimity and rarity and becomes more and more one word among other words as the word of the innumerable encyclicals, decrees and addresses—one word in the discussion of all the questions of the day and which for this reason also allows itself to be more than ever an object of discussion, in a tone that gives friendly counsel (not commands) and offers mater-

nal help (not paternal coercion). In this way, everything achieves an equilibrium on the deeper stra-
tum of the Church's existence, in keeping with a
deeper law: a seemingly excessive burden on the
hierarchical element leads by itself to an encour-
agement of the democratic, while, for the one who
comes into contact with it, taking the democratic
element seriously leads at once and without fail to a
personal choice, demand and mission in the sense
of the ecclesial apostolate in the world.

For both parts of the Church, however, the
teaching and the listening parts, reflection on this
common ecclesial ground is nothing more than
reflection on the most traditional truth, just as Paul
requires that every Christian should realize in daily
living what he has long been in his essence, bringing the "should" into harmony with the already-
existent "is". The externalization of the relationship to the Church for an overwhelming majority
of the Church's members, such as one can see over
long centuries, can therefore only be seen as an
obscuring of the authentic and original state of
affairs, and the overcoming of this situation can
only be seen as the expulsion of a foreign body.

But now we must look back to the first-
mentioned element of the development: the
descent of the Church into contact with the world.
The fact that the Church was initially led in this
descent where she did not wish to go (Jn 21:18)
and that this occurred as a suffering and a humilia-

tion for her, does not alter the fact that she took a very good path carefully planned by Providence. This path has brought her into contact with the world, interiorly, in terms of her destiny, in an awesome solidarity which is quite new in her experience. She, the "closed garden", the "sealed-up spring", the veiled Bride of the thousand monasteries, has been opened up by force and almost ravaged, now that the feet of the nameless multitudes tramp heavily through her soul. Not only have the enclosures of individual monasteries opened up to the new "religious life in the world", where now only the individual heart is an invisible enclosure, but a wall has collapsed in the heart of the Church herself, and where previously only stone seemed to meet the touch of the voluntarily cloistered nun, there is now warm and living flesh: the flesh of the unknown brother who sleeps and dwells, works, suffers and dies in the next room. The Nun Church must learn not to be alarmed at this proximity. And she must learn to preserve the exclusiveness of her relationship to Christ the Bridegroom even through this proximity, indeed to find this relationship anew and more deeply precisely through this proximity.

If from now on there is no longer any Christian "private existence" in the world (since our earth no longer has any space, externally and still less internally, for hermits), this is true also for the Church's sensibility. But it is not the Church as such that trembles at this exposure of her heart, robbed of every protective covering, for the Mediatrix of all graces never lived other than in such an exposure. It is only the individual who shudders—the individual in whom is awakening a sense of the Church which accords with a sense of the present time. He shudders because his own heart is so unfathomable, because the light of ecclesial existence is lighting up his own depths more and more boundlessly, and he shudders because words are sounding in those depths, words coming out of eternity and reverberating down all the labyrinthine passageways of his humanity, and it is impossible to say where these waves of light and sound will ultimately come to rest.

And bastions of the soul are still falling, and the more bastions that fall, the more interconnecting rooms come into existence. Previously, inner and outer were separated: there was the sacred interior space, the profane exterior. According to Augustine, the way led from outer to inner and thence to God: from the externality of the world to the internality of the Church, of the soul; from the deed to contemplation, from a dust-carrying contact with "you" to the bliss of solitude with the "I"—alone at last and recollected in contentment, and able to turn its attention to the marvel and the mystery of God. This path is still viable, but it has been rendered more difficult by the fact that the one who seeks God in the inner room encounters once again the outer realm: the "you", the arena of the profane, and it is only together with all the brethren and all the creatures that he can come before the one God: Father, Son and Spirit.

Earlier too, the orders were separated: the order of creation, where God is generally and universally proclaimed, and the order of redemption and Church, with its particular path leading through Word and grace. It was possible, at least in thought, to pass cleanly over the threshold separating them. But here too, walls have fallen; and although the order of creation and the order of redemption, the world and the Church, must always remain distinct, still we hear anew the words about Christ as the Alpha and Omega of creation—he who recapitulates in himself everything in heaven and on earth and indeed was chosen for this before the world began: namely, to bring back to the Father the world that was created through him, for him, and in him. He himself is not the world, but if he is younger than the world into which he descended and whose nature and being he accepted, nevertheless he is at the same time older than the world; in a mysterious sense it was made according to his archetype, and for the one who knows and understands how to hold up to the light what is, the watermark of Christ shines out, even in the most formal laws of being.

And for a long time, the last and highest wall had been set up between God and the world, so that one who wished to turn to God had to turn away from the world for a time or for ever. This final wall too is collapsing. And although God's sacred being can never be confused with one or with the totality of his creatures, nevertheless God does not wish to become visible to us other than in the context of his creatures: even in the eternal beatitude in which we shall see him face to face, our vision will not be a worldless vision. In all things, as Ignatius intended, we are to find God, who wishes to reveal himself and give himself to us in everything.

The Chinese Wall is being demolished today; we must accept this with regret. What the Wall was meant to say, no longer holds good. God himself broke down yet higher separating walls when his Son appeared, "in order to make out of the two one new man in himself, establishing peace" (Eph 2:15). Tumbling walls can bury much that seemed alive as long as they protected it; but the contact with the space that then comes into being is something greater.